The Dino Grimoire

The Dino Grimoire

Matthew Petchinsky

The Dino Grimoire: Secrets of Prehistoric Magick
By: Matthew Petchinsky

Introduction

Magick is an ancient practice, stretching across the ages, adapting, evolving, and merging with the essence of life. From the earliest shamans who invoked the spirits of the wild to modern practitioners shaping reality with intention, magick has always sought to connect humanity to the unseen forces of the universe. Yet, there is an untapped reservoir of power that predates written history, myth, and ritual—a force born in the primordial age of Earth's greatest creatures: the dinosaurs.

When the world was new and untamed, the land, sky, and sea were teeming with colossal beings that embodied raw elemental energies. These creatures were more than mere animals; they were vessels of natural power, their spirits entwined with the fabric of Earth itself. From the ferocity of the Tyrannosaurus Rex to the serene resilience of the Brachiosaurus, these creatures hold archetypal energies that resonate with the core aspects of existence—strength, survival, transformation, and balance.

Why Prehistoric Magick?

The energy of the prehistoric world is unlike any other. It is untouched by modern influence, preserved in the fossils, the Earth's crust, and the stories whispered through time. When you engage with prehistoric magick, you are accessing a source of power that is pure and primal. This magick is not bound by the complexities of human society or modern constructs; it speaks directly to the soul, awakening the instinctual and intuitive self.

Prehistoric magick bridges the gap between ancient Earth and modern practitioners. By working with this magick, you will tap into:

- **Primordial Strength:** Channel the raw power of creatures that dominated the Earth for millions of years.
- **Elemental Connection:** Align yourself with the forces that shaped the planet—fire, water, earth, and air.
- **Timeless Wisdom:** Unlock the secrets of survival, adaptation, and transformation preserved in fossils and ancient lore.
- **Spiritual Guidance:** Forge relationships with dinosaur spirit guides who offer protection, insight, and empowerment.

The Role of Dinosaurs in Magick

Dinosaurs are more than extinct creatures; they are spiritual symbols of endurance, evolution, and harmony with the natural world. Each species carries unique energies that can be invoked for specific purposes. For example, the cunning and agility of raptors can aid in strategic thinking, while the protective energy of the Stegosaurus can shield you from harm.

These ancient beings also serve as bridges to the Earth's memory. Their fossils hold the imprint of eons, resonating with the vibrations of the prehistoric world. By working with fossils, you can access this timeless energy and infuse your magickal practice with unparalleled potency.

What You'll Learn in This Grimoire

This grimoire is a comprehensive guide to the world of prehistoric magick. Each chapter delves into a specific aspect of this ancient practice, offering practical tools and rituals to integrate its power into your life. You will learn to:

- Identify and work with dinosaur spirit guides.
- Use fossils as talismans and tools for spellcraft.
- Perform rituals inspired by the Jurassic and Cretaceous periods.
- Channel the energies of specific dinosaurs for protection, healing, courage, and transformation.
- Build altars and sacred spaces dedicated to prehistoric magick.
- Explore the symbolic significance of dinosaurs in myth and lore.

Who Is This Grimoire For?

Whether you are an experienced practitioner seeking to expand your magickal repertoire or a curious beginner drawn to the mystique of the prehistoric past, this grimoire will guide you. It is for those who feel a pull toward the ancient and the primal, those who wish to reconnect with the Earth's origins and awaken the wild magick within themselves.

A Journey Through Time and Magick

As you embark on this journey, remember that magick is a partnership. The Earth and its energies will guide you, but your intention and commitment will shape the path. The prehistoric magick within this book is not to be taken lightly—it is raw, transformative, and deeply personal.

This is your invitation to step back in time, to walk alongside the giants of the past and draw from their immense power. With each ritual, spell, and meditation, you will awaken a deeper connection to the Earth and its ancient secrets.

Let **The Dino Grimoire** be your guide as you unearth the mysteries of prehistoric magick. The ancient world is calling—are you ready to answer?

Chapter 1: The Origins of Prehistoric Magick
The Birth of Magick in the Prehistoric World

Long before humanity emerged to weave its own stories, the Earth pulsed with raw, unbridled energy. Volcanoes erupted, oceans roared, and the land teemed with colossal creatures. This was a time when nature existed in its purest form, governed not by human intention but by the primal forces of creation, destruction, and transformation. These forces, untouched by civilization, were the first seeds of magick—the unseen currents that shaped the prehistoric world.

Magick in the prehistoric era was not practiced by humans, as we know it today. Instead, it was an intrinsic part of existence. Every creature, plant, and element carried its own energy, harmonizing to create a living, breathing tapestry of power. Dinosaurs, the dominant life forms of this era, embodied these energies in unique ways. Their massive physical presence, coupled with their instinctual connection to the Earth, made them vessels of pure magickal potential.

As the Earth evolved and life adapted, the echoes of this primordial magick became embedded in its fabric. Fossils, the remnants of this ancient world, act as conduits, preserving the vibrations of this raw energy and making it accessible to modern practitioners.

Understanding Prehistoric Energy

At its core, prehistoric energy is elemental. It is tied to the forces that shaped the Earth in its earliest days:

- **Fire:** The volcanic eruptions that birthed new lands and forged the Earth's crust.
- **Water:** The primordial oceans that nurtured life and carved the landscape.
- **Earth:** The fertile soil and mountains that sustained the first ecosystems.
- **Air:** The vast, unpolluted skies that carried storms and winds of transformation.

These elements were not abstract concepts but tangible, overwhelming presences in the prehistoric world. Dinosaurs, as creatures of this time, interacted with these elements daily, embodying their strength and resilience. For example, the Pterodactyl soared through the skies, representing freedom and vision, while the Stegosaurus, grounded and sturdy, symbolized protection and endurance.

Prehistoric magick draws directly from these elemental forces, amplified by the primal energies of dinosaurs and their environments. When practitioners align themselves with these energies, they tap into a reservoir of power that is both ancient and transformative.

The Connection to Modern Practitioners

Why should a modern-day practitioner explore prehistoric magick? The answer lies in its purity and accessibility. While other forms of magick often require intricate rituals and tools, prehistoric magick relies on intention and connection to the Earth. It invites practitioners to return to the basics, to strip away the complexities of modern life and embrace the primal forces that still exist beneath the surface.

Fossils, for instance, serve as a bridge between the prehistoric past and the present. Holding a fossil connects you to the energy of the Earth as it was millions of years ago. Meditating with a dinosaur tooth or bone fragment allows you to channel the spirit of that creature, gaining insights and strength from its ancient wisdom.

Modern practitioners can also draw inspiration from the survival instincts of dinosaurs. Their ability to adapt, thrive, and evolve despite harsh conditions offers valuable lessons for navigating challenges in today's world. By aligning with these energies, you can cultivate resilience, creativity, and a deeper connection to the natural world.

Foundational Principles of Prehistoric Magick

To work with prehistoric magick, it is essential to understand its foundational principles:

1. **Connection to the Earth:** Prehistoric magick is deeply rooted in the physical world. Practitioners must ground themselves, attuning their energy to the vibrations of the Earth. Walking barefoot, meditating outdoors, or holding a fossil are simple ways to establish this connection.

2. **Reverence for Ancient Energy:** This form of magick respects the power of time and the wisdom carried through eons. Acknowledge the ancient spirits and energies you are working with, honoring their strength and resilience.

3. **Simplicity and Intuition:** Prehistoric magick does not require elaborate tools or rituals. Instead, it encourages practitioners to rely on their intuition, drawing power from the elements, fossils, and the spirits of dinosaurs.

4. **Elemental Focus:** Work with the four primary elements—fire, water, earth, and air—as they were foundational to the prehistoric world. Each element represents a different aspect of life and magick, offering unique energies to channel.

5. **Dinosaur Archetypes:** Understand the symbolic meanings of different dinosaurs and how their traits can enhance your magick. For example, the ferocity of the T-Rex can be invoked for protection, while the wisdom of the Brachiosaurus can aid in healing rituals.

Channeling Prehistoric Energy

Channeling prehistoric energy requires mindfulness and intention. Here are steps to begin:

1. **Create a Sacred Space:** Dedicate an area of your home or an outdoor space to prehistoric magick. Include fossils, stones, and representations of dinosaurs to enhance the energy.
2. **Ground Yourself:** Stand barefoot on the ground, feeling the Earth beneath you. Close your eyes and imagine roots growing from your feet, anchoring you to the prehistoric past.
3. **Invoke Dinosaur Spirits:** Speak aloud or silently call upon a specific dinosaur spirit, such as the Stegosaurus for protection or the Velociraptor for agility. Visualize the dinosaur standing beside you, sharing its energy.
4. **Use Fossils as Conduits:** Hold a fossil in your hands and focus on its texture and weight. Imagine the energy of the ancient world flowing through it and into your body.
5. **Work with the Elements:** Light a candle (fire), place a bowl of water (water), scatter soil or stones (earth), and burn incense (air) to represent the prehistoric elements. Meditate on their presence and power.

Bringing Prehistoric Magick into Everyday Life

Incorporating prehistoric magick into your daily life strengthens your connection to its energies. Here are some simple practices:

- Wear a fossil necklace or carry a small fossil in your pocket for daily protection and grounding.
- Invoke dinosaur spirits during meditation or before challenging tasks to draw on their strength and wisdom.
- Create elemental rituals inspired by the prehistoric world, such as lighting a candle to honor volcanic energy or using seawater in cleansing spells.

The Legacy of Prehistoric Magick

The origins of magick lie in the heart of the Earth, shaped by the creatures and forces that came before us. By embracing prehistoric magick, you honor the planet's history and its enduring power. This ancient energy is a reminder that magick is not confined to time—it is eternal, evolving alongside the Earth and its inhabitants.

As you continue your journey through this grimoire, remember that you are not only learning about prehistoric magick—you are becoming a part of its story, carrying its legacy into the future. Let the wisdom of the past guide you as you step into the transformative power of The Dino Grimoire.

Chapter 2: Connecting with Dinosaur Spirit Guides

Throughout history, spirit guides have been revered as teachers, protectors, and sources of insight. While many practitioners are familiar with animal spirit guides, few realize that the spirits of dinosaurs—ancient, powerful, and primal—can serve as potent allies in the magickal realm. Connecting with these prehistoric guides can help you tap into their unique energies, unlocking strength, resilience, and ancient wisdom.

What Are Dinosaur Spirit Guides?

Dinosaur spirit guides are the spiritual essences of the great creatures that once roamed the Earth. Unlike ancestral or animal guides tied to the human timeline, dinosaur guides embody the primordial energy of a time when nature was wild and unrestrained. They are ancient archetypes, representing pure instinct, adaptability, and raw elemental power.

Each species of dinosaur carries its own symbolic meaning and unique energy. For instance:

- **Tyrannosaurus Rex (T-Rex):** Strength, dominance, and protection.
- **Triceratops:** Grounding, stability, and defense.
- **Pterodactyl:** Freedom, perspective, and higher vision.
- **Velociraptor:** Agility, strategy, and quick thinking.
- **Brachiosaurus:** Patience, endurance, and nurturing energy.
- **Stegosaurus:** Shielding, resilience, and calm determination.

By working with dinosaur spirit guides, you can draw on these attributes to enhance your magickal practice and personal growth.

The Role of Dinosaur Spirit Guides in Prehistoric Magick

Dinosaur spirit guides can serve multiple roles in your magickal journey:

1. **Protectors:** Their immense size and power make them natural guardians against negative energies and psychic attacks.
2. **Teachers:** Dinosaur spirits embody the wisdom of survival and adaptation, teaching lessons about resilience and transformation.
3. **Energy Amplifiers:** These guides can help you channel prehistoric energy more effectively, strengthening your spells and rituals.
4. **Companions:** Like other spirit guides, dinosaurs offer comfort and support, reminding you of your connection to the Earth's history.

Identifying Your Dinosaur Spirit Guide

Finding your dinosaur spirit guide is a personal and intuitive process. While some practitioners may feel drawn to a specific species, others might need to explore and allow the guide to reveal itself. Here are steps to help you identify your guide:

1. Meditation

- Sit in a quiet space where you won't be disturbed.
- Close your eyes and visualize a lush prehistoric landscape. See the trees, rivers, and skies as they would have appeared millions of years ago.
- Invite your dinosaur guide to appear. Say aloud or think:
  "I call upon the dinosaur spirit guide who aligns with my highest good. Reveal yourself to me."
- Be patient and observe. You may see a specific dinosaur, sense its energy, or hear its name in your mind.

2. Dreams

Dinosaur spirit guides often appear in dreams. Before going to sleep, set an intention to meet your guide by saying:

"As I dream tonight, I invite my dinosaur spirit guide to show itself to me."

Pay attention to any dinosaurs or prehistoric imagery that appears in your dreams. Keep a journal to record your experiences and impressions.

3. Signs and Synchronicities

Your dinosaur spirit guide might reveal itself through signs in your daily life. For example:

- Repeated sightings of fossils or dinosaur imagery.
- A strong fascination with a particular species.
- Feeling a connection when reading about a specific dinosaur.

Trust your intuition and follow the trail of synchronicities.

4. Divination

Use divination tools like tarot cards, pendulums, or runes to ask which dinosaur spirit guide is aligned with you. For example, you can create a spread where each card represents a different species and see which card is drawn.

Working with Dinosaur Spirit Guides

Once you have identified your guide, building a relationship with it is essential. This connection strengthens over time as you honor and engage with its energy.

1. Build an Altar

Create a sacred space dedicated to your dinosaur spirit guide. Include:

- Fossils or fossil replicas.
- Images or figurines of the dinosaur.
- Candles, crystals, and items that resonate with the dinosaur's elemental energy (e.g., volcanic stones for T-Rex, feathers for Pterodactyl).

Spend time at the altar meditating, making offerings, or simply sitting in quiet reflection.

2. Offerings

Offerings show respect and gratitude to your guide. Suitable offerings include:

- Natural items like stones, plants, or water.
- Symbolic items such as bones, fossil-like trinkets, or drawings of your guide.
- Acts of service, like cleaning up a natural area, which honors the Earth they once roamed.

3. Invoke Their Presence

Before rituals or meditations, invite your guide to join you by saying:

"I call upon [Name of Dinosaur Spirit], my guide and ally, to lend your strength and wisdom to this working."

Feel their energy surround you and amplify your practice.

4. Dreamwork and Journeying

Work with your guide in the dreamscape or through shamanic journeying. Visualize yourself walking beside your guide in a prehistoric landscape. Ask questions, seek advice, or simply observe their movements and behavior.

5. Use Their Symbolism in Spells

Incorporate your guide's traits into your spellwork. For example:

- Invoke the T-Rex for protection spells.
- Call on the Velociraptor for strategic planning and swift action.
- Work with the Stegosaurus for shielding against negativity.

Include images, fossils, or sigils of your guide to strengthen the spell.

Symbolism and Energies of Key Dinosaur Spirit Guides

Here's a deeper look at the unique traits and energies of some common dinosaur spirit guides:

- **Tyrannosaurus Rex (T-Rex):** A symbol of dominance and strength, the T-Rex is an excellent guide for protection, courage, and leadership. Its ferocity can help you overcome challenges and assert your power.
- **Triceratops:** Known for its sturdy, defensive nature, the Triceratops represents grounding, stability, and protection. Call on this guide when you need to shield yourself from harm or build a solid foundation.
- **Pterodactyl:** This winged guide embodies freedom, perspective, and vision. It is ideal for astral projection, travel, and gaining clarity in confusing situations.
- **Velociraptor:** Agile and intelligent, the Velociraptor symbolizes cunning, strategy, and adaptability. This guide is perfect for problem-solving and quick decision-making.
- **Brachiosaurus:** A gentle giant, the Brachiosaurus brings patience, endurance, and nurturing energy. It is an excellent ally for healing and long-term projects.
- **Stegosaurus:** The Stegosaurus represents resilience and calm determination. Its energy is ideal for shielding and grounding practices.
- **Ankylosaurus:** With its armored body and clubbed tail, the Ankylosaurus is a protector against psychic attacks and negativity. It offers steadfast resilience in the face of adversity.

Strengthening Your Bond

Building a strong connection with your dinosaur spirit guide requires consistency and respect. Regularly meditate, make offerings, and acknowledge your guide's presence in your daily life. Over time, you'll find that their energy becomes an integral part of your magickal practice, providing guidance, protection, and empowerment.

Working with dinosaur spirit guides is a powerful way to access the ancient, untamed energy of the prehistoric world. Their wisdom is timeless, their power immense, and their presence a reminder of the enduring connection between the past and the present. Embrace their guidance as you journey deeper into the mysteries of **The Dino Grimoire.**

Chapter 3: The Magick of Fossils

Fossils are more than remnants of a long-lost world; they are portals to the prehistoric Earth, holding the vibrational imprint of ancient energies. These preserved fragments of life—bones, shells, leaves, and even imprints—are talismans of immense power. To the magickal practitioner, fossils serve as keys to accessing the primordial energy of the Jurassic, Cretaceous, and other prehistoric periods. They act as bridges, connecting us to the raw and unrefined forces that shaped the planet millions of years ago.

What Are Fossils?

Fossils are the mineralized remains or impressions of ancient organisms. Over millennia, organic material is replaced by minerals, creating a permanent record of life that existed in the distant past. They are formed through processes such as permineralization, casts and molds, carbonization, and preservation in amber. Each fossil carries not only the essence of the organism it represents but also the geological history of the Earth at the time of its formation.

For magickal purposes, fossils are more than scientific artifacts. They are sacred objects infused with the energy of time, transformation, and survival. Each fossil is a testament to the resilience of life and the cycles of creation and destruction that govern the natural world.

The Energetic Properties of Fossils

Fossils are imbued with unique magickal properties derived from their origins. These properties make them versatile tools in spellwork, divination, and meditation. Key attributes include:

1. **Timeless Energy:** Fossils resonate with the energy of the prehistoric Earth, offering access to ancient wisdom and primal power.
2. **Transformation:** The process of fossilization itself represents transformation, making fossils potent symbols for personal growth and change.
3. **Stability and Grounding:** Fossils, particularly those formed in sedimentary rock, are deeply connected to the Earth, providing grounding and stability in magickal practices.
4. **Protection:** As remnants of creatures that once ruled the Earth, fossils can serve as talismans for protection, invoking the strength and resilience of the prehistoric world.
5. **Connection to Prehistoric Spirits:** Fossils act as conduits for connecting with dinosaur spirit guides and other ancient energies.

Types of Fossils and Their Magickal Uses

Different types of fossils carry distinct energies, which can be harnessed for specific purposes:

- **Dinosaur Bones:** Symbolizing strength, courage, and endurance, these fossils are ideal for protection spells and rituals focused on overcoming obstacles.
- **Ammonites:** These spiral-shaped fossils represent cycles, transformation, and cosmic energy. They are excellent for meditations on life's patterns and transitions.
- **Amber:** Fossilized tree resin, amber is a powerful conduit for preserving energy and protecting against negativity. It is also associated with solar energy and vitality.
- **Petrified Wood:** Representing grounding, stability, and patience, petrified wood is perfect for connecting with Earth energies and anchoring spiritual practices.
- **Fossilized Shark Teeth:** These fossils carry the energy of adaptability and primal instincts, making them useful for spells related to survival and resourcefulness.
- **Trilobites:** As some of the oldest known fossils, trilobites embody ancient wisdom and are excellent tools for accessing deep knowledge and enhancing intuition.

How to Use Fossils in Magick

Fossils can be incorporated into magickal practices in a variety of ways, depending on your intention and the type of fossil you are working with. Below are some of the most effective methods for harnessing their power:

1. Fossils as Talismans

- Carry a fossil in your pocket or wear it as jewelry to benefit from its protective and grounding energy throughout the day.
- Place fossils on your altar to amplify the prehistoric energy in your sacred space.

2. Fossils in Spells and Rituals

- **Protection Spells:** Use dinosaur bones or ammonites to create a protective barrier around yourself or your home. Arrange them in a circle and visualize their energy forming a shield.
- **Transformation Rituals:** Incorporate petrified wood or ammonites into rituals for personal growth and change. Meditate on the fossil's energy, envisioning it guiding you through a transformative process.
- **Healing Spells:** Amber is particularly effective in healing rituals. Hold a piece of amber over the affected area and visualize its warm, golden energy restoring balance and vitality.

3. Fossils in Divination

Fossils can be used as tools for divination, offering insights into the past, present, and future. For example:

- Hold a fossil in your hand during meditation and ask it to reveal messages or visions.
- Use a pendulum made from fossil material to answer questions or guide decision-making.

4. Fossil Grids

Create an energy grid using fossils to amplify your intentions. Arrange fossils in geometric patterns on your altar, with each type of fossil representing a specific energy or goal. For example:

- Ammonites at the center for transformation.
- Petrified wood at the corners for grounding.
- Amber for protection and healing.

5. Fossil Meditation

Meditating with fossils can help you connect with the prehistoric Earth and its energies. To begin:

- Hold a fossil in your dominant hand or place it on your third eye.
- Close your eyes and visualize the world as it was when the organism lived. Picture dinosaurs roaming, ancient oceans, or vast forests.
- Allow the fossil's energy to guide your thoughts and reveal insights.

Fossil Care and Cleansing

Fossils are powerful tools, but like any magickal object, they require care and cleansing to maintain their energy. Here are some tips:

1. **Physical Care:**
   - Handle fossils with care, as they can be fragile.
   - Store them in a safe, dry place to prevent damage.
2. **Energetic Cleansing:**
   - **Smoke Cleansing:** Pass the fossil through the smoke of sage, palo santo, or incense to clear any stagnant energy.
   - **Moonlight:** Place fossils under the light of the full moon to recharge their energy.
   - **Earth Cleansing:** Bury the fossil in soil for 24 hours to reconnect it with the Earth's energy.
3. **Charging Fossils:**
   - Place fossils on your altar or in sunlight (if the fossil type is not light-sensitive) to recharge them.
   - Set an intention while holding the fossil, infusing it with your specific goal or desire.

Prehistoric Altars and Fossil Integration

Creating a prehistoric-themed altar is an excellent way to honor fossils and integrate their energy into your practice. Here's how to design one:

1. **Choose a Sacred Space:** Select a dedicated area for your altar, such as a table or shelf.
2. **Incorporate Fossils:** Arrange fossils in a meaningful pattern, perhaps aligning them with the elements or directions.
3. **Add Elemental Tools:** Include items that represent the four elements (candles, water, stones, feathers) to balance the prehistoric energy.
4. **Include Dinosaur Imagery:** Add figurines, drawings, or carvings of dinosaurs to deepen the connection.
5. **Set Your Intention:** Dedicate the altar to prehistoric magick, stating your intention aloud or silently.

The Magickal Legacy of Fossils

Fossils are timeless artifacts that bridge the gap between the prehistoric past and the present. They are tangible reminders of the Earth's resilience, adaptability, and cycles of change. By incorporating fossils into your magickal practice, you align yourself with these enduring qualities, drawing strength and inspiration from the ancient world.

The magick of fossils is a testament to the power of nature and the lessons it offers. As you continue to work with these ancient talismans, you will find that their energy not only enhances your practice but also deepens your connection to the Earth's history and its eternal mysteries. Let fossils be your guide as you journey through **The Dino Grimoire** and unlock the secrets of prehistoric magick.

Chapter 4: Rituals of the Jurassic Era

The Jurassic Era, spanning approximately 201 to 145 million years ago, was a time of immense transformation and flourishing life. The Earth was lush with vast forests, towering ferns, and vibrant ecosystems, creating an environment teeming with energy. Dominated by colossal dinosaurs like the Brachiosaurus, Stegosaurus, and Allosaurus, this era embodies the principles of growth, stability, resilience, and the power of nature's cycles.

Harnessing the energies of the Jurassic Era through ritual practice allows modern magickal practitioners to tap into this fertile, primal power. These rituals celebrate growth, transformation, strength, and harmony with the natural world.

The Energies of the Jurassic Era

To understand and work with the magick of the Jurassic Era, it is essential to connect with its elemental and symbolic energies:

1. **Growth and Expansion:** The Jurassic period saw a dramatic proliferation of life, symbolizing abundance and fertility.
2. **Resilience and Strength:** The dinosaurs of this era evolved and thrived amidst changing environments, embodying adaptability and survival.
3. **Earth and Nature:** Towering plants, ancient forests, and volcanic activity made this period rich in Earth energy.
4. **Cycles of Life:** The Jurassic Era reflects the cycles of creation, destruction, and renewal that govern all life.

Each of these energies can be invoked in rituals to enhance personal growth, build resilience, or deepen your connection to nature.

Preparing for Jurassic Rituals

Before performing Jurassic-inspired rituals, proper preparation is key to aligning with the energies of this ancient period:

1. **Sacred Space Setup:**
    - Create an altar or ritual space decorated with natural elements such as ferns, stones, and wooden objects.
    - Include fossils or representations of Jurassic creatures (figurines, images, or sigils).
    - Use green, brown, and deep earthy tones to reflect the lush environment of the Jurassic world.
2. **Elemental Focus:**
    - **Earth:** Incorporate soil, stones, or petrified wood.
    - **Fire:** Represent volcanic activity with candles or a small bonfire (if outdoors).
    - **Water:** Use a bowl of water to symbolize ancient rivers and lakes.
    - **Air:** Add feathers or incense to invoke the expansive Jurassic skies.
3. **Attunement:** Meditate to visualize the Jurassic landscape. Imagine standing in a prehistoric forest surrounded by towering trees and hearing the distant calls of dinosaurs. Ground yourself in this visualization to establish a connection with the era's energy.

Rituals of the Jurassic Era

1. Ritual of Abundance: Calling the Spirit of the Brachiosaurus

The Brachiosaurus, one of the most iconic creatures of the Jurassic Era, symbolizes growth, abundance, and patience. This ritual invokes its energy to attract prosperity and cultivate long-term success.

Materials Needed:

- A green candle (for abundance)
- A piece of petrified wood or fossil
- A small bowl of seeds (symbolizing growth)

Steps:

1. Light the green candle and place it on your altar. Surround it with the petrified wood and the bowl of seeds.
2. Close your eyes and visualize a Brachiosaurus walking gracefully through a prehistoric forest, its long neck reaching toward the treetops.
3. Recite: *"Brachiosaurus, gentle giant of growth,*
   I call upon your strength and patience both.
   Bring abundance, steady and sure,
   Prosperity that will long endure."
4. Take the seeds and scatter them in your garden or a natural area as an offering, symbolizing your intention to grow abundance in your life.

2. Ritual of Protection: Invoking the Stegosaurus Shield

The Stegosaurus, with its formidable plates and tail spikes, embodies resilience and protection. This ritual creates a psychic shield to safeguard against negativity and harm.

Materials Needed:

- A black or brown candle (for protection)
- A small stone or crystal (e.g., obsidian or black tourmaline)
- A bowl of salt

Steps:

1. Place the stone and bowl of salt on your altar. Light the candle.
2. Visualize a Stegosaurus standing guard beside you, its plates forming a barrier of protection.
3. Sprinkle the salt in a circle around your ritual space while chanting: *"Stegosaurus, guardian strong,*
   Protect me from all that is wrong.
   Your shield defends, your power holds,
   Keep me safe, brave and bold."
4. Carry the stone with you as a talisman of protection, infused with the Stegosaurus's energy.

3. Ritual of Strength: Harnessing the Allosaurus's Power

The Allosaurus, a fearsome predator of the Jurassic, symbolizes raw strength and determination. This ritual is designed to bolster courage and help you overcome challenges.

Materials Needed:

- A red candle (for strength and vitality)
- A fossilized tooth or a sharp stone
- A small drum or instrument (optional)

Steps:

1. Light the red candle and hold the fossil or sharp stone in your hand.
2. Beat the drum or clap your hands rhythmically to evoke the energy of the Allosaurus.
3. Chant: *"Allosaurus, hunter bold,*
   Grant me strength, fierce and untold.
   With your power, I will stand,
   Unshaken, steady, strong, and grand."
4. Visualize the Allosaurus lending you its strength, its roar resonating through your being. Carry the fossil or stone as a token of this energy.

4. Ritual of Renewal: The Jurassic Flame

Volcanic activity was a hallmark of the Jurassic Era, symbolizing destruction followed by renewal. This ritual channels volcanic energy to release old patterns and welcome transformation.

Materials Needed:

- A red and orange candle
- A small cauldron or fireproof bowl
- Paper and pen

Steps:

1. Write down anything you wish to release (fears, habits, or obstacles) on the paper.
2. Light the candles and visualize a prehistoric volcano erupting, its lava cleansing the land and making way for new growth.
3. Place the paper in the cauldron or bowl and safely burn it, saying: *"Jurassic flames, fierce and bright,*
   Burn away the dark of night.
   From destruction, new life grows,
   Transformation's fire flows."
4. Scatter the ashes outdoors as a symbol of letting go and embracing change.

5. Ritual of Connection: Walking with Jurassic Spirits

This ritual deepens your bond with the spirit guides of the Jurassic Era, inviting their wisdom and energy into your life.

Materials Needed:

- Fossils or representations of Jurassic dinosaurs
- A blue candle (for connection and insight)
- A feather or small branch

Steps:

1. Place the fossils and the candle on your altar. Light the candle.
2. Hold the feather or branch and visualize walking through a Jurassic forest. Imagine dinosaurs appearing around you, their energy radiating wisdom and power.
3. Say: *"Spirits of the Jurassic past,*
   I call on your wisdom, ancient and vast.
   Walk with me, teach and guide,
   Be my allies, by my side."

4. Sit in meditation, observing any impressions or messages that come through. Record your experiences in a journal.

Integrating Jurassic Rituals into Your Practice

The rituals of the Jurassic Era are designed to harness the transformative power of this ancient time. To deepen your connection, incorporate elements of Jurassic energy into your daily life:

- Meditate with fossils or representations of Jurassic creatures.
- Spend time in nature, focusing on the cycles of growth and renewal.
- Reflect on the resilience and adaptability of Jurassic life when facing personal challenges.

By working with these rituals, you not only honor the legacy of the Jurassic Era but also awaken its timeless energies within yourself. Through this connection, you become a steward of prehistoric magick, carrying its wisdom into the present day.

Chapter 5: Channeling the Power of the T-Rex

The Tyrannosaurus Rex, often called the "King of the Dinosaurs," embodies raw strength, dominance, and unyielding power. With its massive size, sharp teeth, and commanding presence, the T-Rex ruled the prehistoric world as a symbol of survival and primal energy. In magickal practice, the T-Rex represents protection, leadership, courage, and the ability to face challenges head-on. By invoking the energy of this ancient predator, practitioners can channel its might to overcome obstacles, shield themselves from harm, and assert their personal power.

The Symbolism of the T-Rex in Magick

The T-Rex carries profound symbolic meaning that resonates with modern practitioners seeking to harness its energy:

1. **Protection:** As a top predator, the T-Rex had no natural enemies, symbolizing ultimate protection from external threats.
2. **Strength:** Its sheer physical power makes the T-Rex a potent symbol of resilience and endurance.
3. **Leadership:** The T-Rex's dominance in the prehistoric ecosystem reflects its role as a natural leader and authority figure.
4. **Courage:** The T-Rex fearlessly pursued its goals, embodying the bravery needed to confront challenges.
5. **Primal Instinct:** Tapping into the T-Rex's energy awakens the practitioner's instincts, encouraging decisive action and heightened awareness.

Preparing to Work with T-Rex Energy

Before invoking the T-Rex's power, it's essential to align yourself with its energy. This requires grounding, focus, and creating a sacred space that reflects its primal essence.

1. Setting the Scene

- Decorate your altar or ritual space with items symbolizing the T-Rex's energy: bones, fossils, volcanic stones, and predator imagery.
- Use colors like red, black, and gold to represent strength, protection, and dominance.
- Burn earthy or spicy incense, such as dragon's blood or sandalwood, to evoke the T-Rex's primal power.

2. Grounding and Centering

The T-Rex's energy is rooted in the Earth, so grounding is a crucial step. Stand barefoot on the ground (if possible) and visualize roots extending from your feet into the Earth's core. Imagine yourself drawing strength and stability from the planet.

3. Connecting with the Spirit of the T-Rex

Meditate on the image of a T-Rex in its natural habitat. Picture it walking through a prehistoric forest, exuding confidence and power. Envision this mighty creature approaching you, its energy merging with yours. Feel its strength filling your body and mind.

Rituals to Channel the Power of the T-Rex
1. Ritual of Protection: The T-Rex's Shield
This ritual creates a powerful protective barrier around you, invoking the T-Rex's energy to ward off harm and negativity.
Materials Needed:

- A black candle (for protection)
- A small fossil or bone (optional, for focus)
- A bowl of salt

Steps:

1. Light the black candle and place the bowl of salt on your altar.
2. Hold the fossil or bone in your hands (if using) and visualize the T-Rex standing behind you, its massive form creating a shield.
3. Sprinkle the salt in a circle around your ritual space while chanting:
   "Tyrannosaurus Rex, protector and king,
   Shield me from harm, let no danger bring.
   With your strength and power, fierce and true,
   Guard me now, as I call upon you."
4. Imagine the T-Rex's protective energy forming a barrier around you, solid and impenetrable.
5. Carry the fossil or a small pouch of salt as a talisman of protection.

2. Ritual of Strength: Harnessing the T-Rex's Power

This ritual is designed to channel the T-Rex's strength and resilience, empowering you to face challenges and achieve your goals.

Materials Needed:

- A red candle (for strength and vitality)
- A piece of volcanic stone or hematite
- A drawing or figurine of the T-Rex

Steps:

1. Place the T-Rex image or figurine on your altar as a focal point.
2. Light the red candle and hold the volcanic stone or hematite in your hand.
3. Close your eyes and visualize the T-Rex roaring, its energy surging through your body, filling you with strength.
4. Chant:
   "T-Rex, mighty and strong,
   Your power I channel, fierce and long.
   With every step, with every breath,
   I claim your strength, beyond all death."
5. Allow the energy to flow through you, empowering your body, mind, and spirit. Carry the stone as a talisman of strength.

3. Ritual of Leadership: Commanding the T-Rex's Presence

Invoke the T-Rex's energy to enhance confidence, assertiveness, and leadership abilities in situations where you need to take charge.

Materials Needed:

- A gold candle (for authority and confidence)
- A feather or piece of amber (optional, for focus)
- A mirror

Steps:

1. Light the gold candle and place the feather or amber on your altar.
2. Stand in front of the mirror and look into your own eyes. Visualize the T-Rex standing tall and regal behind you, its energy radiating through you.
3. Say:
   "King of dinosaurs, ruler of all,
   Grant me confidence, I stand tall.
   With your might, I lead with grace,
   Guiding others in my rightful place."
4. Imagine yourself embodying the T-Rex's commanding presence, speaking and acting with authority and confidence.
5. Carry the feather or amber with you as a reminder of your leadership energy.

4. Ritual of Courage: Facing Challenges with the T-Rex's Strength

When fear or doubt threatens to overwhelm you, this ritual calls on the T-Rex's fearless spirit to embolden you.

Materials Needed:

- A red and black candle (for courage and protection)
- A fossil or sharp stone
- A piece of paper and pen

Steps:

1. Write down the challenge or fear you wish to overcome on the paper.
2. Light the candles and place the fossil or sharp stone on your altar.
3. Visualize the T-Rex roaring, its strength dissolving your fear. Feel its courage infusing your body and mind.
4. Say:
   "T-Rex, fearless and bold,
   Your courage I summon, my strength to hold.
   With your roar, my fear is gone,
   I rise with power, I carry on."
5. Burn the paper (safely) in the candle flame as a symbol of releasing your fear. Scatter the ashes outdoors.

T-Rex Sigils and Symbols

Create a sigil inspired by the T-Rex to enhance your connection to its energy. Draw a symbol combining sharp angles (representing its teeth) and strong lines (representing its strength). Use this sigil in your rituals, carve it into candles, or carry it as a talisman.

Daily Practices to Strengthen Your Bond

1. **Meditate on the T-Rex's Image:** Spend a few minutes each day visualizing the T-Rex and feeling its energy surround you.
2. **Wear Fossil Jewelry:** Carry a fossilized tooth or piece of amber as a constant reminder of the T-Rex's power.
3. **Incorporate Roaring Affirmations:** Begin your day with affirmations spoken boldly, imagining the roar of the T-Rex amplifying your words.

Embodying the T-Rex's Power in Everyday Life

Channeling the T-Rex's energy is not limited to rituals; it's about embodying its strength and confidence in your daily actions. Approach challenges with courage, stand firm in your decisions, and remember that you carry the spirit of a ruler within you. The T-Rex reminds us that true power lies in embracing our inner strength and asserting it with unwavering confidence.

Let the might of the T-Rex guide you as you navigate life's challenges, always reminding you of the primal, unstoppable force that resides within. **The Dino Grimoire** will continue to reveal the mysteries of prehistoric magick as you grow stronger, protected by the King of the Dinosaurs.

Chapter 6: The Wisdom of the Triceratops

The Triceratops, a three-horned, herbivorous dinosaur from the late Cretaceous period, is a symbol of resilience, grounding, and stability. Known for its sturdy frame, defensive horns, and iconic frill, this dinosaur navigated a world filled with predators while maintaining its calm, steadfast presence. In magickal practice, the Triceratops represents grounded strength, the ability to stand firm against adversity, and the wisdom to protect what is sacred.

By connecting with the energy of the Triceratops, practitioners can enhance their own resilience, create stability in chaotic situations, and develop protective barriers for their physical and spiritual well-being. This chapter explores how to invoke the wisdom of the Triceratops and integrate its grounding energy into your magickal practice.

The Symbolism of the Triceratops

The Triceratops carries powerful symbolic meanings that align with its behavior and characteristics:

1. **Grounding and Stability:** With its massive body and low center of gravity, the Triceratops embodies balance and rootedness.
2. **Resilience:** Its thick hide, frill, and horns symbolize the ability to withstand challenges and recover from setbacks.
3. **Defense and Protection:** The Triceratops's horns and frill were used both for defense and display, representing the importance of protecting oneself and one's boundaries.
4. **Gentle Strength:** Despite its power, the Triceratops was an herbivore, symbolizing peaceful strength and the ability to coexist harmoniously while remaining prepared for confrontation.

The Energetic Attributes of the Triceratops

The Triceratops's energy is deeply connected to the Earth and its cycles. It resonates with the following qualities:

- **Elemental Earth Energy:** As a creature that thrived on plants and stayed close to the ground, the Triceratops is a strong conduit for grounding and connecting with Earth's energy.
- **Protective Magick:** Its defensive horns and frill make the Triceratops a natural ally in spells for shielding and guarding against negativity.
- **Endurance:** The Triceratops teaches perseverance, helping you navigate long-term challenges with strength and grace.

Preparing to Work with Triceratops Energy

Before invoking the Triceratops's wisdom, it is essential to prepare yourself and your ritual space to align with its grounding energy.

1. Create a Sacred Space

- Decorate your altar or ritual area with earthy tones, stones, and plants.
- Include fossils, wooden objects, or representations of the Triceratops (figurines, images, or sigils).
- Use green and brown candles to evoke the grounding and stabilizing energy of the Earth.

2. Gather Elemental Tools

- **Earth:** A stone or crystal such as hematite, black tourmaline, or petrified wood.
- **Water:** A bowl of spring water to symbolize the Triceratops's connection to life-sustaining nourishment.
- **Air:** Feathers or incense to honor its harmonious presence in nature.
- **Fire:** A small flame to represent the resilience and inner power of the Triceratops.

3. Ground Yourself

Grounding is essential when working with Triceratops energy. Stand barefoot on the ground, close your eyes, and visualize roots growing from your feet into the Earth. Feel the stability and strength of the Earth anchoring you in the present moment.

Rituals to Invoke the Wisdom of the Triceratops
1. Ritual for Grounding: Embracing Earth's Energy
This ritual connects you to the grounding energy of the Triceratops, helping you stay balanced and centered during times of stress or uncertainty.
Materials Needed:

- A green candle
- A piece of petrified wood or a smooth river stone
- A bowl of soil

Steps:

1. Place the green candle, petrified wood or stone, and bowl of soil on your altar. Light the candle.
2. Hold the petrified wood or stone in your hands and close your eyes. Visualize a Triceratops walking steadily through a prehistoric forest, calm and grounded.
3. Say:
   "Triceratops, steady and strong,
   Root me where I belong.
   Ground my spirit, balance my soul,
   Help me stay present, complete, and whole."
4. Place the stone on the soil and leave it there for a day to solidify your grounding energy.

2. Ritual for Resilience: Strength Through Challenges

Invoke the Triceratops's resilience to help you endure difficult times and overcome obstacles with grace.

Materials Needed:

- A brown candle
- A piece of obsidian or black tourmaline
- A drawing or figurine of a Triceratops

Steps:

1. Light the brown candle and place the obsidian on your altar.
2. Visualize the Triceratops standing in front of you, its thick hide deflecting all harm and its horns ready to defend against threats.
3. Chant:
   "Triceratops, ancient and wise,
   Teach me to endure, to rise.
   With your strength, I shall prevail,
   Through any storm, I will not fail."
4. Hold the obsidian and envision it absorbing the Triceratops's resilience. Carry the stone with you as a talisman of endurance.

3. Ritual for Protection: The Triceratops Shield

This ritual uses the Triceratops's defensive energy to create a spiritual shield, protecting you from negativity and harm.

Materials Needed:

- A black or dark green candle
- A circle of stones or salt
- A small fossil or piece of hematite

Steps:

1. Arrange the stones or salt in a circle around your ritual space to symbolize the Triceratops's frill as a protective barrier.
2. Light the black or green candle and hold the fossil or hematite.
3. Visualize the Triceratops forming a shield around you, its frill deflecting all harm. Say:
   "Triceratops, with horns held high,
   Guard me from dangers passing by.
   Shield me with your ancient might,
   Keep me safe both day and night."

4. Leave the fossil or hematite on your altar as a token of protection.

4. Ritual for Balance: Harmonizing Body and Spirit

Call upon the Triceratops to bring balance and harmony into your life, ensuring stability in both physical and spiritual aspects.

Materials Needed:

- Two candles (one green, one white)
- A feather or leaf
- A small bowl of water

Steps:

1. Light the green and white candles, placing the feather or leaf between them.
2. Hold the bowl of water in your hands and visualize the Triceratops moving gracefully through its environment, balanced and steady.
3. Chant:
   "Triceratops, keeper of balance true,
   Teach me the harmony of old and new.
   Help me align, steady and strong,
   Guide me to where my soul belongs."
4. Pour the water onto the Earth as an offering, symbolizing the balance you seek.

Triceratops Sigils and Talismans

Design a sigil inspired by the Triceratops to focus its energy in your rituals. Incorporate shapes like triangles (representing its horns) and circles (representing its frill) into the design. Use this sigil in protective spells, carve it into candles, or wear it as a talisman.

Daily Practices to Strengthen Your Connection

1. **Meditate with Fossils or Stones:** Hold a piece of petrified wood or hematite during meditation to channel the Triceratops's grounding energy.
2. **Visualize the Triceratops:** Spend time each day visualizing the Triceratops walking beside you, offering its strength and protection.
3. **Adopt Grounding Rituals:** Practice grounding techniques like walking barefoot outdoors or spending time in nature to stay aligned with the Triceratops's energy.

Embodying the Triceratops's Wisdom in Life

The Triceratops teaches us the importance of staying grounded, building resilience, and protecting what matters most. By embracing its wisdom, you can navigate life's challenges with calm determination and unshakable strength. The lessons of this gentle giant remind us that true power lies in balance—between standing firm and moving forward, between defense and coexistence.

Through the guidance of the Triceratops, you will discover the strength to endure, the wisdom to protect, and the resilience to thrive in any situation. Let its energy be your ally as you journey deeper into **The Dino Grimoire** and the ancient magick of the prehistoric world.

Chapter 7: Pterodactyl Sky Magick

The Pterodactyl, an ancient flying reptile from the late Jurassic period, embodies freedom, perspective, and mastery of the skies. Although not technically a dinosaur, the Pterodactyl was a pioneering force in the prehistoric skies, its wings spanning vast distances and symbolizing exploration and transcendence. In magickal practice, the energy of the Pterodactyl offers a gateway to higher realms, aiding in astral projection, vision quests, and expanding spiritual horizons.

By connecting with the Pterodactyl, practitioners can unlock their potential to soar beyond physical and spiritual limitations, gaining clarity, insight, and freedom of thought.

The Symbolism of the Pterodactyl

The Pterodactyl's symbolism is deeply tied to its mastery of the skies and its ability to traverse vast distances. Key attributes include:

1. **Freedom:** The Pterodactyl represents liberation from constraints, whether physical, emotional, or spiritual.
2. **Perspective:** Its high vantage point allows it to see the broader picture, making it a symbol of clarity and understanding.
3. **Exploration:** As a creature of the air, the Pterodactyl embodies curiosity and the courage to venture into the unknown.
4. **Spiritual Ascension:** The ability to fly connects the Pterodactyl to the spirit world, making it a powerful guide for astral travel and vision work.

The Energetic Attributes of the Pterodactyl

The Pterodactyl's energy is dynamic and expansive, resonating with the following qualities:

- **Air Element:** It is deeply aligned with the element of air, representing intellect, intuition, and communication.
- **Expansive Energy:** Its wingspan symbolizes the ability to reach far and wide, both physically and spiritually.
- **Guidance in the Higher Realms:** As a creature of flight, the Pterodactyl serves as a bridge between the physical and astral planes.

Preparing to Work with Pterodactyl Energy
1. Sacred Space Preparation
Create a ritual space that reflects the energy of flight and the skies:

- Use light, airy colors like blue, white, and silver.
- Decorate your altar with feathers, sky-related imagery, or representations of the Pterodactyl.
- Incorporate incense or essential oils with airy or uplifting scents, such as lavender, eucalyptus, or frankincense.

2. Grounding and Centering
Although Pterodactyl energy is expansive, grounding yourself before working with it ensures balance. Visualize roots extending from your feet into the Earth, anchoring you as you prepare to ascend.

3. Visualizing the Pterodactyl
Meditate to visualize a Pterodactyl soaring above you. Imagine its powerful wings creating currents of energy that lift you upward. Feel its wisdom and freedom entering your aura.

Rituals for Pterodactyl Sky Magick

1. Flight-Based Spells: Enhancing Freedom and Mobility

This ritual calls upon the Pterodactyl's energy to help you break free from constraints or achieve physical or metaphorical movement in your life.

Materials Needed:

- A white or silver candle
- A feather or wing-shaped object
- A piece of clear quartz

Steps:

1. Light the candle and place the feather or quartz on your altar.
2. Hold the quartz in your hand and visualize yourself soaring through the skies alongside a Pterodactyl. Feel the wind carrying you higher, breaking free from limitations.
3. Say:
   "Pterodactyl, master of flight,
   Guide my wings through day and night.
   Free me from chains, lift me high,
   Teach me to soar, reach for the sky."
4. Carry the quartz as a talisman to remind you of your freedom and mobility.

2. Astral Projection: Soaring Beyond the Physical Realm

The Pterodactyl is an excellent guide for astral projection, helping you travel safely and gain insights from other realms.

Materials Needed:

- A blue candle (for spiritual travel)
- A piece of moonstone or amethyst
- A comfortable space for meditation

Steps:

1. Light the blue candle and hold the moonstone or amethyst in your hand.
2. Lie down in a comfortable position and close your eyes. Visualize a Pterodactyl swooping down to meet you, offering its wings as a vehicle for astral travel.
3. Chant:
   "Pterodactyl, take me beyond,
   To realms unknown, where I belong.

Wings of wisdom, guide my flight,
Safely through the astral night."

4. Allow the Pterodactyl to lift you into the astral plane. Explore the visions and messages you receive, and when ready, visualize it returning you safely to your body.
5. Record your journey in a journal.

3. Vision Quests: Gaining Clarity and Insight

This ritual invokes the Pterodactyl to provide clarity and insight into your life's challenges or decisions.

Materials Needed:

- A white or gold candle
- A bowl of water
- A piece of labradorite or aquamarine

Steps:

1. Light the candle and place the bowl of water on your altar, with the labradorite beside it.
2. Sit comfortably and gaze into the water's surface, imagining a Pterodactyl circling above you. Its keen eyesight allows it to see clearly, even from great heights.
3. Chant:
"Pterodactyl, soaring high,
Lend me your sight to clarify.
Show me the truth, clear and bright,
Guide my visions, day and night."
4. Continue gazing into the water, allowing images or messages to form. Write down any insights you receive.

4. Expanding Spiritual Horizons: The Wings of Wisdom

This ritual is designed to help you expand your spiritual awareness and connect with higher realms of understanding.

Materials Needed:

- A silver or light blue candle
- A feather or a piece of sky-blue cloth
- A piece of celestite or angelite

Steps:

1. Light the candle and hold the celestite or angelite in your hand.
2. Close your eyes and visualize yourself standing at the edge of a prehistoric cliff. A Pterodactyl lands beside you, spreading its wings as an invitation to explore higher realms.
3. Chant:
"Pterodactyl, wise and free,
Lift my spirit, let me see.
Higher realms, where truths reside,
Guide me there, be my guide."
4. Imagine yourself soaring through the skies with the Pterodactyl, gaining new spiritual insights. When ready, return to the present moment and journal your experience.

Pterodactyl Sigils and Talismans

Design a sigil that embodies the energy of the Pterodactyl. Incorporate wing-like shapes and flowing lines to symbolize flight and freedom. Use this sigil in your rituals, draw it on candles, or wear it as a charm to enhance your connection to the Pterodactyl's energy.

Daily Practices to Strengthen Your Connection

1. **Meditation with Feathers or Crystals:** Hold a feather or a sky-blue crystal during meditation to align with the Pterodactyl's energy.
2. **Spend Time in Open Spaces:** Visit areas with wide-open skies, such as hilltops or open fields, to connect with the expansive energy of flight.
3. **Visualize Flight:** Close your eyes and imagine yourself soaring through the skies like a Pterodactyl, free and unburdened.

Embodying Pterodactyl Sky Magick in Life

The Pterodactyl reminds us to rise above challenges, seek new perspectives, and embrace freedom in all aspects of life. By working with its energy, you can navigate life's obstacles with clarity and grace, always keeping your eyes on the horizon.

Through the guidance of the Pterodactyl, you will discover the limitless possibilities of the skies, expanding your spiritual practice and enhancing your magickal abilities. Let its wisdom and freedom inspire you as you journey deeper into **The Dino Grimoire**, unlocking the ancient secrets of prehistoric magick.

Chapter 8: Stegosaurus Shields

The Stegosaurus, with its iconic plates and spiked tail, is a symbol of steadfast defense and grounded resilience. This herbivorous dinosaur from the Jurassic period relied on its physical defenses to deter predators, and in the magickal realm, it inspires the creation of spiritual shields to protect against psychic attacks, negative energies, and emotional harm. The Stegosaurus embodies calm determination and the power to guard oneself without aggression, making it an ideal archetype for defensive magick.

In this chapter, you will learn how to draw on the energy of the Stegosaurus to create powerful spiritual shields, defend your personal energy, and cultivate an aura of resilience.

The Symbolism of the Stegosaurus

The Stegosaurus offers rich symbolism that aligns with its physical attributes and behavior:

1. **Protection:** Its plated back and spiked tail symbolize the ability to shield oneself from harm while maintaining a calm and peaceful presence.
2. **Grounded Strength:** As a creature closely tied to the Earth, the Stegosaurus represents stability and resilience.
3. **Defense Without Aggression:** The Stegosaurus teaches us to protect ourselves without unnecessary confrontation, relying on our inner strength and boundaries.
4. **Balance:** The dual nature of its defenses—plated armor for shielding and spikes for action—represents a balance between passive and active protection.

The Energetic Attributes of the Stegosaurus

When working with Stegosaurus energy, you connect to these powerful traits:

- **Earth Element:** Deeply tied to the Earth, the Stegosaurus is a grounding force that strengthens your connection to stability and resilience.
- **Aura Shielding:** Its plates inspire the creation of protective barriers around your aura, guarding against energetic intrusions.
- **Psychic Defense:** Its spiked tail symbolizes active defense, helping you repel psychic attacks or negative influences.

Preparing to Work with Stegosaurus Energy
1. Create a Stegosaurus-Inspired Sacred Space
Design a ritual space that reflects the grounded and protective energy of the Stegosaurus:

- Use earthy tones like green, brown, and gold.
- Incorporate stones such as obsidian, black tourmaline, or hematite for grounding and protection.
- Add imagery or figurines of the Stegosaurus to represent its energy.
- Use incense or oils with earthy scents, such as patchouli, cedarwood, or vetiver, to create a grounded atmosphere.

2. Ground Yourself
The Stegosaurus is closely tied to the Earth, so grounding is essential before invoking its energy. Stand barefoot on the ground (if possible) and visualize roots extending from your feet deep into the Earth, anchoring you securely.

3. Meditate on the Stegosaurus
Spend time meditating on the image of a Stegosaurus. Visualize its plated back as a protective barrier and its spiked tail as a tool for repelling threats. Invite its energy to merge with yours, filling you with a sense of calm strength and readiness.

Rituals to Create Stegosaurus Shields
1. Aura Shielding Ritual: Building the Plate Barrier
This ritual uses the energy of the Stegosaurus to create a protective aura shield, guarding you from negative energies and psychic attacks.
Materials Needed:

- A black or brown candle (for protection and grounding)
- A piece of obsidian or black tourmaline
- A small bowl of salt

Steps:

1. Light the candle and place the obsidian or black tourmaline and bowl of salt on your altar.
2. Close your eyes and visualize the Stegosaurus standing behind you, its plates radiating protective energy that surrounds your aura.
3. Sprinkle the salt in a circle around your space, chanting:
   "Stegosaurus, shield of might,
   Protect my soul both day and night.
   Plates of strength, surround and guard,
   Keep me safe from harm and hard."
4. Imagine your aura glowing with a shield of energy, impenetrable and resilient. Carry the obsidian or black tourmaline as a talisman to maintain the shield.

2. Psychic Defense Ritual: Activating the Spiked Tail
This ritual focuses on actively repelling psychic attacks and banishing negative influences using the symbolism of the Stegosaurus's spiked tail.
Materials Needed:

- A red candle (for strength and banishment)
- A sharp object or crystal (e.g., a quartz point or dagger-shaped stone)
- A mirror

Steps:

1. Light the red candle and place the sharp object or crystal on your altar.
2. Sit in front of the mirror and visualize the Stegosaurus's spiked tail swinging in a powerful arc, cutting through any negative energy around you.
3. Say:
   "Stegosaurus, tail of defense,

Repel all harm, drive out offense.
With your spikes, my space you clear,
No ill shall linger, none shall near."

4. Visualize the spikes creating a barrier of light that banishes negativity. Carry the sharp object or crystal as a tool for continued protection.

3. Ritual for Home Protection: Stegosaurus Sanctuary

This ritual creates a protective energy barrier around your home, inspired by the Stegosaurus's plated back.

Materials Needed:

- Four stones (one for each corner of your home or space)
- A green candle (for harmony and protection)
- A small bowl of water

Steps:

1. Place the stones in the four corners of your home or space.
2. Light the green candle and hold the bowl of water, visualizing the Stegosaurus standing guard at each corner, its plates forming a protective perimeter.
3. Chant:
   "Stegosaurus, guardian true,
   Protect this home in all I do.
   Plates of strength and grounding light,
   Guard this space both day and night."
4. Sprinkle a few drops of water on each stone, sealing the protective energy. Leave the stones in place as protective anchors.

4. Ritual for Emotional Resilience: Strength of the Plates

This ritual helps you build emotional resilience and maintain inner peace during challenging times.

Materials Needed:

- A white candle (for clarity and peace)
- A piece of amethyst or rose quartz
- A small bowl of soil

Steps:

1. Light the white candle and hold the amethyst or rose quartz in your hands.

2. Place the bowl of soil on your altar and visualize the Stegosaurus walking calmly through its environment, undisturbed by external chaos.
3. Chant:
   "Stegosaurus, calm and wise,
   Teach me strength that never dies.
   Plates of peace and heart of stone,
   Help me stand, steady and alone."
4. Place the soil in a plant or garden as an offering of gratitude. Carry the stone as a token of resilience.

Stegosaurus Sigils and Talismans

Create a sigil inspired by the Stegosaurus's energy. Use triangular shapes (representing its plates) and spiked patterns to symbolize its protective qualities. Carve this sigil into candles, draw it on paper, or wear it as a talisman to enhance your connection to the Stegosaurus.

Daily Practices to Strengthen Your Connection

1. **Meditate with Protective Stones:** Hold stones like obsidian, hematite, or black tourmaline to channel the Stegosaurus's energy into your daily practice.
2. **Walk Barefoot on the Earth:** Connect with the Earth to ground yourself, just as the Stegosaurus maintained its connection to its environment.
3. **Visualize Shields:** Regularly visualize the Stegosaurus's plated back surrounding you, reinforcing your spiritual defenses.

Embodying Stegosaurus Energy in Life

The Stegosaurus teaches us that true strength lies in resilience and preparedness. By embodying its wisdom, you can navigate life's challenges with grace and confidence, knowing you are protected and grounded. Whether facing emotional turmoil, psychic attacks, or everyday stress, the Stegosaurus reminds us to stand firm, guard our boundaries, and protect our inner peace.

Let its energy guide you as you journey deeper into **The Dino Grimoire**, building spiritual shields that ensure your safety and resilience in all aspects of life.

Chapter 9: Raptor Agility and Strategy Spells

Raptors, particularly Velociraptors, are among the most iconic dinosaurs, revered for their agility, intelligence, and cunning. Known for their sharp minds and coordinated hunting strategies, raptors symbolize quick thinking, adaptability, and precision in action. By channeling the energy of these prehistoric predators, practitioners can enhance their decision-making skills, sharpen their instincts, and achieve success in situations requiring strategy and agility.

This chapter delves into the magick of raptors, offering rituals and spells to harness their traits for success in both mundane and magickal endeavors.

The Symbolism of Raptors

The Velociraptor and its relatives carry profound symbolic meanings, reflecting their unique abilities and behaviors:

1. **Cunning and Intelligence:** Raptors relied on their sharp minds and strategic hunting techniques, symbolizing cleverness and tactical thinking.
2. **Agility and Speed:** Their swift movements and precise actions embody adaptability and the ability to react quickly to changing circumstances.
3. **Coordination and Teamwork:** Raptors are often associated with collaboration, teaching the importance of working with others to achieve a common goal.
4. **Predatory Focus:** Raptors' intense focus and determination make them symbols of ambition and the drive to succeed.

The Energetic Attributes of Raptors

Raptors exude a unique energy that resonates with traits essential for success in strategy, combat, and decision-making:

- **Mental Clarity:** Raptors' intelligence aligns with sharp thinking and problem-solving.
- **Precision:** Their ability to strike with accuracy mirrors the importance of calculated actions in magick and life.
- **Adaptability:** Raptors' agility represents the power to adjust and thrive in dynamic environments.
- **Ambition:** Their predatory nature symbolizes the drive to pursue goals relentlessly.

Preparing to Work with Raptor Energy
1. Create a Sacred Space
Design a ritual space that reflects the energy of raptors:

- Use sharp, focused colors like red, black, and silver.
- Decorate your altar with feathers, claw-like objects, or fossils.
- Burn incense or essential oils with invigorating scents, such as cinnamon, rosemary, or eucalyptus, to enhance focus and clarity.

2. Ground and Center Yourself
Before working with raptor energy, ground yourself to ensure balance. Visualize roots extending from your feet into the Earth, anchoring you, while your upper body remains light and ready for action.

3. Visualize the Raptor
Meditate on the image of a Velociraptor moving gracefully through its environment. Imagine its sharp claws, keen eyes, and swift movements, embodying its energy as you prepare for the rituals.

Rituals and Spells for Raptor Agility and Strategy
1. Quick Thinking Spell: The Raptor's Mind
This spell enhances mental clarity and quick decision-making, helping you navigate challenges with intelligence and precision.
Materials Needed:

- A silver candle (for mental sharpness)
- A feather or small claw-like object (real or symbolic)
- A piece of clear quartz

Steps:

1. Light the silver candle and place the feather or claw-like object and quartz on your altar.
2. Hold the quartz in your hand and visualize a Velociraptor stalking its prey, calculating every step with precision.
3. Chant:
   "Raptor keen and mind so bright,
   Grant me clarity, insight, and light.
   Help me think with cunning and speed,
   Guide my mind in times of need."
4. Carry the quartz as a talisman for enhanced mental clarity.

2. Strategy Ritual: Mapping the Raptor's Path
Invoke the raptor's strategic energy to plan and execute goals effectively.
Materials Needed:

- A black candle (for focus and ambition)
- A piece of paper and pen
- A small fossil or stone (optional, for grounding)

Steps:

1. Light the black candle and place the fossil or stone on your altar.
2. Write your goal on the paper, breaking it down into smaller, actionable steps. Visualize a raptor stalking its prey, each movement deliberate and calculated.
3. Say:
   "Velociraptor, strategy supreme,
   Teach me to map my path, my dream.
   Step by step, I shall proceed,
   With your wisdom, I will succeed."
4. Keep the paper in a safe place and review it regularly as you work toward your goal.

3. Agility Enhancement Spell: The Raptor's Swiftness

This spell channels the agility of raptors to enhance physical and mental adaptability, allowing you to thrive in changing environments.

Materials Needed:

- A red candle (for speed and vitality)
- A piece of carnelian or tiger's eye
- A feather or lightweight object

Steps:

1. Light the red candle and hold the carnelian or tiger's eye in your hand.
2. Visualize a raptor darting through its environment, swift and graceful. Feel its energy flowing into you, sharpening your reflexes and adaptability.
3. Chant:
   "Raptor swift, your speed I claim,
   Grant me agility, sharp as flame.
   Through life's changes, I shall move,
   Quick and steady, in rhythm, smooth."
4. Carry the stone as a talisman to maintain this energy in your daily life.

4. Combat and Defense Ritual: The Raptor's Claw

Use this ritual to invoke raptor energy for defense and success in confrontational or competitive situations.

Materials Needed:

- A black and red candle (for protection and power)
- A sharp object or claw-like symbol (real or symbolic)
- A mirror

Steps:

1. Light the black and red candles, placing the sharp object or claw on your altar.
2. Stand before the mirror and visualize a Velociraptor standing behind you, its claws and teeth ready to defend and strike.
3. Chant:
   "Velociraptor, predator wise,
   Defend my ground, no harm shall rise.
   Strike with precision, guard my domain,
   Your strength flows through me, none shall remain."

4. Hold the sharp object or claw as a talisman during situations requiring defense or assertiveness.

Daily Practices to Strengthen Your Connection

1. **Meditate on Raptor Imagery:** Visualize raptors in their natural habitat, focusing on their grace and intelligence.
2. **Carry Symbols of Raptors:** Wear or carry items like feathers, claw-shaped jewelry, or small fossils to stay attuned to their energy.
3. **Practice Reflex Training:** Engage in activities that enhance your physical or mental agility, such as mindfulness exercises or quick decision-making games.

Sigils and Talismans for Raptor Energy

Design a sigil inspired by the raptor's agility and strategy. Incorporate sharp angles (representing claws) and flowing lines (symbolizing swift movement). Use this sigil in spells or carve it into candles for added focus.

Embodying Raptor Energy in Daily Life

The raptor's energy is not just for rituals—it's a mindset. Embody its traits by approaching challenges with precision, maintaining focus under pressure, and adapting quickly to new circumstances. Use its cunning and strategy to navigate complex situations and its agility to overcome obstacles with ease.

Through the guidance of raptors, you can sharpen your instincts, elevate your strategic thinking, and enhance your decision-making abilities. Let the energy of these prehistoric predators inspire you to thrive as you journey deeper into **The Dino Grimoire**, mastering the magick of agility and strategy.

Chapter 10: The Magick of Dinosaur Eggs

Dinosaur eggs are among the most captivating relics of the prehistoric world. These ancient symbols of life and potential hold immense magickal significance, representing creation, fertility, rebirth, and the cyclical nature of existence. In magickal practice, dinosaur eggs can be used to inspire growth, nurture new ideas, and manifest creation in both physical and spiritual realms.

This chapter explores the symbolic and mystical significance of dinosaur eggs and provides rituals, spells, and meditative practices to incorporate their energy into your magickal workings.

The Symbolism of Dinosaur Eggs

Dinosaur eggs, like all eggs, symbolize the beginning of life, but their connection to the prehistoric world imbues them with unique meanings:

1. **Creation and Fertility:** Eggs are universal symbols of creation, embodying the potential for new life and growth. Dinosaur eggs, in particular, connect to the Earth's earliest life forms, making them potent symbols of primal creation.
2. **Rebirth and Renewal:** Just as eggs hatch into new life, they symbolize transformation and the renewal of energy, whether in a project, relationship, or personal growth.
3. **Nurturing and Protection:** Eggs represent the protective environment needed to foster life, highlighting the importance of care and patience during periods of growth.
4. **Infinite Potential:** An egg holds the promise of what it will become, making it a powerful representation of untapped possibilities and creative energy.

The Energetic Attributes of Dinosaur Eggs

Dinosaur eggs resonate with unique energies that reflect their prehistoric origins and universal symbolism:

- **Primordial Life Energy:** They carry the essence of Earth's earliest cycles of life, offering a connection to primal creative forces.
- **Grounded Creation:** Unlike abstract symbols of creation, dinosaur eggs are deeply tied to the Earth, grounding creative energies in reality.
- **Transformation:** The process of hatching represents the journey from potential to actualization, making them powerful tools for manifestation.

Incorporating Dinosaur Egg Energy into Magick

Dinosaur eggs, whether real fossils or symbolic representations, can be used in various ways to enhance your magickal practice:

1. Symbolic Representations

- Use replica dinosaur eggs or other egg-shaped stones and objects to represent dinosaur eggs in rituals.
- Crystals like moonstone, selenite, or quartz shaped into eggs carry both the symbolism of eggs and their own unique properties.

2. Altar Decor

- Place dinosaur eggs or their representations on your altar to focus on creation and fertility energy.
- Surround the egg with elements that reflect your intention, such as plants for growth or candles for transformation.

3. Meditation Tool

- Hold a dinosaur egg fossil or a symbolic egg during meditation to connect with its energy and visualize its potential for creation and growth.

Rituals and Spells Using Dinosaur Eggs
1. Fertility Spell: Invoking Life's Potential
This spell channels the energy of dinosaur eggs to enhance fertility, whether physical, creative, or metaphorical.
Materials Needed:

- A green candle (for fertility and growth)
- A dinosaur egg fossil or egg-shaped crystal (e.g., moonstone)
- A small bowl of soil

Steps:

1. Light the green candle and place the egg and bowl of soil on your altar.
2. Hold the egg in your hands and visualize it glowing with vibrant, life-giving energy. Imagine this energy expanding and filling your body or your creative project.
3. Chant:
   "Egg of life, ancient and true,
   Grant me the power to create anew.
   With fertile ground and nurturing care,
   Life and growth, I now declare."
4. Bury the bowl of soil in a garden or pot to symbolize planting the seeds of your intention. Keep the egg on your altar as a talisman of fertility.

2. Creation Ritual: Manifesting Ideas and Dreams

This ritual uses dinosaur egg energy to manifest creative projects, new beginnings, or innovative ideas.

Materials Needed:

- A white candle (for purity and creation)
- A piece of paper and pen
- A dinosaur egg representation (fossil, crystal, or symbolic egg)

Steps:

1. Light the white candle and place the egg in front of it.
2. Write your intention or idea on the piece of paper, focusing on what you wish to create or bring to life.
3. Hold the egg in your hands and visualize your idea taking shape, growing within the egg like an embryo.
4. Say:
   "From this egg, creation flows,
   A seed of life that grows and grows.
   My dream takes form, my will be done,
   The journey of creation has begun."
5. Place the paper under the egg on your altar and revisit it regularly as your intention manifests.

3. Rebirth Ritual: Embracing Transformation
This ritual focuses on using dinosaur egg energy to release old patterns and embrace renewal.
Materials Needed:

- A black candle (for release)
- A white candle (for new beginnings)
- A dinosaur egg or symbolic egg
- A bowl of water

Steps:

1. Light the black candle to symbolize the release of old energy. Hold the egg and focus on what you wish to let go of, imagining it being absorbed into the egg.
2. Dip the egg in the bowl of water, symbolizing cleansing and transformation.
3. Light the white candle to represent rebirth. Hold the egg again and visualize it glowing with new, vibrant energy, ready to hatch into a fresh start.
4. Chant:
   "Egg of rebirth, ancient and wise,
   Transform my soul, let new life arise.
   From old to new, I now ascend,
   A cycle complete, a new path begins."
5. Keep the egg as a symbol of your transformation.

4. Nurturing Energy Spell: Building Protective Space
This spell uses the egg's symbolism of protection and nurturing to create a safe and supportive environment for growth.
Materials Needed:

- A brown candle (for grounding and protection)
- A dinosaur egg or egg-shaped stone
- A small plant or seedling

Steps:

1. Light the brown candle and place the egg beside it. Hold the plant or seedling in your hands.
2. Visualize a protective shell forming around you and your goals, nurturing them in a safe environment like the shell of an egg.
3. Chant:
   "Egg of care, nurturing and strong,
   Protect my growth all the day long.

Keep me safe, shield my space,
Let my dreams grow at their own pace."

4. Plant the seedling as a representation of your growth and place the egg near it as a guardian.

Using Dinosaur Eggs in Daily Magick

1. **Meditation Tool:** Hold an egg-shaped stone or fossil during meditation to focus on creation and renewal.
2. **Creative Inspiration:** Keep a symbolic egg on your desk or creative space to inspire new ideas and projects.
3. **Fertility Talisman:** Carry an egg-shaped crystal as a talisman to enhance fertility and the potential for growth.

Sigils and Talismans for Dinosaur Egg Energy

Design a sigil incorporating the shape of an egg to represent creation, protection, or rebirth. Draw this sigil on paper, carve it into candles, or wear it as a charm to enhance your connection to the energy of dinosaur eggs.

Embodying the Energy of Dinosaur Eggs

Dinosaur eggs remind us of the infinite potential within ourselves and the importance of nurturing our ideas and goals. By working with their energy, you can connect to the cycles of creation, release, and renewal, drawing on the wisdom of the prehistoric world to enrich your magickal practice.

Let the ancient power of dinosaur eggs inspire you as you continue your journey through **The Dino Grimoire**, unlocking the mysteries of life, growth, and transformation.

Chapter 11: Prehistoric Elemental Magick

Elemental magick is a cornerstone of many spiritual practices, drawing on the forces of fire, water, earth, and air to create balance, transformation, and power. In prehistoric times, these elements were more than abstract concepts—they were the driving forces that shaped the planet, defined survival, and gave life its rhythm. By tapping into their primordial forms, practitioners can access a deep, primal energy that connects us to the Earth's earliest magickal currents.

This chapter explores the nature of prehistoric elemental magick and provides detailed rituals, tools, and practices to align with these primal forces.

The Nature of Prehistoric Elements

In the prehistoric world, the elements were raw and untamed, shaping the environment and the creatures that lived within it. Each element carried unique qualities and energies that remain accessible today:

1. **Fire:** The volcanic eruptions of the Jurassic and Cretaceous periods symbolized destruction and creation, representing transformation, passion, and raw power.
2. **Water:** Ancient seas and rivers nurtured the first life forms, embodying adaptability, intuition, and cleansing.
3. **Earth:** The solid ground provided stability and nourishment, symbolizing growth, grounding, and resilience.
4. **Air:** Expansive skies carried the breath of life and the winds of change, representing freedom, communication, and spiritual elevation.

When channeled together, these elements create harmony and a profound connection to the Earth's earliest energies.

Elemental Magick Tools and Correspondences
Fire

- **Colors:** Red, orange, gold
- **Symbols:** Lava stones, volcanic imagery, candles
- **Crystals:** Carnelian, pyrite, fire agate
- **Plants:** Cinnamon, chili pepper, sunflower
- **Animals:** Pterodactyl (associated with the fiery skies), predatory dinosaurs (like T-Rex, symbolizing power)

Water

- **Colors:** Blue, teal, silver
- **Symbols:** Shells, fossils of marine life, bowls of water
- **Crystals:** Aquamarine, moonstone, blue calcite
- **Plants:** Water lilies, seaweed, willow
- **Animals:** Plesiosaurs, fish, amphibians

Earth

- **Colors:** Green, brown, black
- **Symbols:** Stones, soil, dinosaur bones
- **Crystals:** Petrified wood, obsidian, hematite
- **Plants:** Ferns, moss, oak
- **Animals:** Stegosaurus (symbolizing grounding), herbivorous dinosaurs

Air

- **Colors:** White, light blue, yellow
- **Symbols:** Feathers, incense, wind chimes
- **Crystals:** Selenite, citrine, celestite
- **Plants:** Sage, eucalyptus, lavender
- **Animals:** Pterosaurs, flying insects

Rituals and Practices for Prehistoric Elemental Magick
1. Fire Ritual: Harnessing Primordial Flames
This ritual connects you to the transformative and passionate energy of prehistoric volcanic activity.
Materials Needed:

- A red or orange candle
- A piece of volcanic stone (e.g., basalt or obsidian)
- A bowl of sand or soil

Steps:

1. Light the candle and place the volcanic stone in the bowl of sand. Visualize a prehistoric volcano erupting, its molten lava both destroying and creating the land.
2. Chant:
   "Primordial fire, fierce and bright,
   Ignite my soul with your burning light.
   Transform my path, renew my flame,
   With your power, I rise again."
3. Meditate on the flame, visualizing it burning away obstacles and igniting your passions. Carry the volcanic stone as a talisman of fiery transformation.

2. Water Ritual: Flowing with Ancient Seas
This ritual aligns you with the cleansing and intuitive energy of prehistoric waters.
Materials Needed:

- A bowl of water
- A shell or fossil of a marine creature
- A blue candle

Steps:

1. Place the bowl of water and shell on your altar. Light the blue candle.
2. Hold the shell or fossil and visualize ancient seas teeming with life, their currents washing over you and cleansing your energy.
3. Chant:
   "Waters of old, deep and wise,
   Cleanse my spirit, open my eyes.
   Let intuition and flow be my guide,
   As I embrace the magick inside."

4. Dip your hands in the water, allowing it to cleanse and refresh you. Use the shell or fossil as a focus for intuition and emotional balance.

3. Earth Ritual: Grounding with Prehistoric Soil

This ritual connects you to the grounding and nourishing energy of the prehistoric Earth.

Materials Needed:

- A piece of petrified wood or bone fossil
- A bowl of soil or clay
- A green candle

Steps:

1. Light the green candle and hold the petrified wood or fossil in your hands. Visualize the Earth as it was during prehistoric times, its rich soil giving life to ancient forests and creatures.
2. Chant:
   "Earth of old, steady and true,
   Ground my spirit, guide me through.
   With your strength, I stand with grace,
   Rooted deeply in time and space."
3. Place your hands in the soil or clay, feeling its grounding energy. Leave the fossil on your altar to maintain this connection.

4. Air Ritual: Embracing Prehistoric Winds

This ritual aligns you with the freedom and clarity of prehistoric skies.

Materials Needed:

- A feather or wind chime
- A piece of celestite or citrine
- A white or yellow candle

Steps:

1. Light the candle and hold the feather or wind chime. Visualize the expansive prehistoric skies, filled with the winds that carried life across the planet.
2. Chant:
   "Winds of change, light and free,
   Carry my spirit, let me see.
   Whisper wisdom, clear my mind,
   With your breath, my truth I find."

3. Gently wave the feather or chime the wind chime, imagining the air clearing away confusion and filling you with clarity. Keep the celestite or citrine nearby to maintain this lightness and vision.

Combining the Elements: The Prehistoric Circle

To fully integrate the power of prehistoric elemental magick, create a ritual that combines all four elements.

Materials Needed:

- A red candle (fire)
- A bowl of water (water)
- A stone or fossil (earth)
- A feather or incense (air)

Steps:

1. Place the items in a circle, with each representing one element. Sit in the center and light the candle and incense.
2. Chant:
   "Elements of ancient days,
   Guide me through your timeless ways.
   Fire, water, earth, and air,
   Teach me balance beyond compare."
3. Meditate on each element, visualizing how they worked together to shape the prehistoric world. Feel their energies combining within you, creating harmony and balance.

Using Prehistoric Elemental Magick in Daily Life

1. **Fire:** Light a candle during moments of transformation to ignite your passions and focus your energy.
2. **Water:** Carry a shell or fossil to stay connected to the intuitive flow of life.
3. **Earth:** Use a piece of petrified wood or bone fossil to ground yourself during stressful situations.
4. **Air:** Hang wind chimes or use a feather in meditative practices to invite clarity and freedom.

Embodying Prehistoric Elemental Energy

Prehistoric elemental magick reminds us that the same forces that shaped the ancient world are still present within and around us. By working with these primal energies, you can ground yourself in the Earth's history while embracing the dynamic potential of fire, water, earth, and air. This practice connects you to the cycles of creation, destruction, and renewal that define both the prehistoric and modern worlds.

Through the guidance of these elements, you can harmonize your magickal practice and life, continuing your journey into **The Dino Grimoire** with a deeper connection to the ancient forces that shaped our planet.

Chapter 12: The Cretaceous Call: Rituals of Transformation

The Cretaceous period, spanning 145 to 66 million years ago, was a time of profound change and evolution. It marked the rise of flowering plants, the dominance of massive dinosaurs like the Tyrannosaurus Rex and Triceratops, and ultimately, the dramatic asteroid impact that transformed the Earth forever. This period embodies cycles of growth, adaptation, and rebirth through transformation. In magick, the energy of the Cretaceous serves as a potent source of inspiration for transformative rituals that guide practitioners through periods of personal change, growth, and renewal.

This chapter explores how the dynamic shifts of the Cretaceous can be channeled into magickal practices to inspire transformation in various aspects of life.

The Symbolism of the Cretaceous Period

The Cretaceous is rich in symbolic meaning, reflecting the powerful forces of evolution and transformation:

1. **Growth and Flourishing:** The emergence of flowering plants and ecological diversity symbolizes growth, innovation, and abundance.
2. **Adaptation:** Dinosaurs of this era thrived in diverse environments, teaching lessons in flexibility and survival.
3. **Cataclysm and Rebirth:** The asteroid impact that ended the Cretaceous represents destruction as a precursor to renewal and new beginnings.
4. **Evolution:** This period's dynamic changes reflect the necessity of evolving to thrive in a changing world.

The Energetic Attributes of the Cretaceous Period

The energy of the Cretaceous is transformative, embodying both creation and destruction. Key energetic traits include:

- **Catalyst for Change:** The Cretaceous energy disrupts the status quo, sparking growth and transformation.
- **Resilience:** The survival and adaptation of life during this period reflect the power of perseverance.
- **Rebirth:** The end of the Cretaceous heralded a new era, symbolizing the cycle of death and renewal.

Preparing to Work with Cretaceous Energy

Before working with the transformative energy of the Cretaceous, prepare your mind, body, and ritual space to align with its dynamic power.

1. Create a Sacred Space

- Use symbols of the Cretaceous period, such as images or figurines of dinosaurs like the T-Rex and Triceratops, fossils, or flowering plants.
- Incorporate colors that reflect transformation, such as green (growth), red (passion and change), and black (rebirth).
- Burn incense or essential oils with grounding yet invigorating scents, such as patchouli, cedarwood, or orange.

2. Ground and Center Yourself

Grounding is crucial to stay balanced during transformative work. Visualize yourself as a flowering plant growing from the prehistoric soil, deeply rooted yet reaching for the sky.

3. Meditate on Cretaceous Change

Meditate on the significant events of the Cretaceous period. Visualize the lush forests, diverse ecosystems, and the asteroid impact that brought a dramatic end, making way for new beginnings. Imagine this energy flowing through you, awakening your power to transform.

Rituals for Transformation Inspired by the Cretaceous
1. Growth and Abundance Ritual: Blooming with Possibilities

This ritual channels the flourishing energy of flowering plants from the Cretaceous to foster growth and abundance in your life.

Materials Needed:

- A green candle (for growth)
- A flowering plant or seeds
- A bowl of soil

Steps:

1. Light the green candle and place the plant or seeds in front of you.
2. Hold the bowl of soil and visualize it as the fertile ground of the Cretaceous period, teeming with life and potential.
3. Chant:
   "From ancient Earth, where blooms took hold,
   Let abundance and growth unfold.
   As seeds of life were born anew,
   May my dreams and goals take root and true."
4. Plant the seeds or place the soil around the flowering plant. Nurture it as a living representation of your intentions for growth.

2. Adaptation Ritual: Embracing Change

This ritual invokes the resilience of Cretaceous creatures to help you navigate life's transitions with strength and adaptability.

Materials Needed:

- A piece of petrified wood or fossil
- A white candle (for clarity and adaptability)
- A bowl of water

Steps:

1. Light the white candle and hold the petrified wood or fossil in your hands.
2. Reflect on a challenge or transition you are facing, visualizing yourself adapting to it as dinosaurs adapted to their changing environments.
3. Chant:
   "Ancient life, both fierce and wise,
   Teach me to adapt, to rise.
   With strength and grace, I'll persevere,
   Through every change, I'll stand sincere."
4. Dip the fossil or wood into the water, symbolizing fluid adaptability. Keep it on your altar or carry it as a talisman.

3. Rebirth Ritual: The Asteroid's Renewal

This ritual focuses on releasing the old and embracing new beginnings, inspired by the asteroid impact that ended the Cretaceous and sparked a new era.

Materials Needed:

- A black candle (for release)
- A white candle (for renewal)
- A piece of obsidian or black tourmaline
- A piece of clear quartz

Steps:

1. Light the black candle and hold the obsidian. Focus on what you wish to release—old habits, fears, or stagnant energy.
2. Chant:
   "Endings come, as cycles do,
   Clear the old, make way for new.
   Like the Earth transformed by flame,
   I rise anew, my path reclaimed."
3. Blow out the black candle and light the white candle. Hold the quartz and visualize new energy filling the space left by what you released.
4. Chant:
   "From destruction, rebirth takes flight,
   A new dawn rises, clear and bright.
   I welcome change, I embrace the new,
   With strength and purpose, I'll follow through."
5. Carry the quartz as a symbol of your rebirth.

4. Evolution Ritual: Stepping into Your Higher Self

This ritual aligns you with the energy of evolution, helping you step into a higher version of yourself.

Materials Needed:

- A red candle (for transformation)
- A piece of amethyst (for spiritual growth)
- A mirror

Steps:

1. Light the red candle and place the amethyst on your altar.
2. Stand before the mirror and visualize your current self evolving into your higher self, shedding doubts and limitations.
3. Chant:
   "Cretaceous growth, fierce and strong,
   Evolve me now, where I belong.
   Shed the old, embrace the new,
   My higher self, I now pursue."
4. Hold the amethyst and affirm your commitment to growth and self-improvement.

Daily Practices to Strengthen Your Connection

1. **Journaling Transformation:** Reflect on your personal growth, noting areas where you have adapted or evolved.
2. **Carry Cretaceous Symbols:** Wear fossils or keep stones like petrified wood to stay connected to the transformative energy of the Cretaceous.
3. **Meditate on Rebirth:** Visualize the asteroid impact as a cleansing force, clearing old energy and making way for new possibilities.

Embodying Cretaceous Energy in Life

The Cretaceous period teaches us that transformation is a natural part of life's cycles. By embracing its energy, you can face challenges with resilience, adapt to changing circumstances, and evolve into the best version of yourself. Let the dynamic forces of this prehistoric era inspire you to release what no longer serves you and step boldly into your future.

Through the guidance of the Cretaceous, you will discover the power of transformation, continuing your journey into **The Dino Grimoire** with renewed strength and purpose.

Chapter 13: Fossil Divination

Fossils are not only remnants of prehistoric life but also potent tools for accessing ancient wisdom and uncovering insights into the past, present, and future. Fossil divination combines the timeless energy of fossils with intuitive practices to help practitioners receive guidance, solve problems, and connect with the cycles of life. Just as fossils preserve the imprints of creatures and plants from millions of years ago, they can reveal imprints of the energies that shape our lives.

This chapter explores how to use fossils in divination, including methods for preparation, interpretation, and rituals to enhance your connection to their energy.

The Power of Fossils in Divination

Fossils are unique divination tools because they hold the essence of time itself. Their formation process imbues them with qualities that are deeply useful in magick and spiritual work:

1. **Connection to the Past:** Fossils act as conduits to ancient knowledge, helping you understand how the past influences the present.
2. **Grounding Energy:** Their earthy nature makes them stable and reliable tools for interpreting complex energies.
3. **Timeless Wisdom:** Fossils bridge the gap between what has been and what is yet to come, offering insights into cycles and patterns.
4. **Resilience and Adaptation:** The survival of these remains through eons symbolizes the power of endurance and transformation, which can be reflected in readings.

Choosing Fossils for Divination

Different types of fossils carry unique energies that can enhance your divination practice. Choose fossils based on your intentions:

- **Ammonites:** Represent cycles, transformation, and evolution. Ideal for readings about life changes and personal growth.
- **Petrified Wood:** Symbolizes grounding, stability, and connection to Earth's wisdom. Perfect for questions about security and balance.
- **Dinosaur Bones:** Represent strength, endurance, and primal energy. Use for readings about challenges and personal power.
- **Fossilized Shells:** Embody protection and emotional resilience. Helpful for exploring relationships and emotional well-being.
- **Trilobites:** Reflect ancient wisdom and adaptability. Best for readings about intellectual growth and problem-solving.

Preparing Fossils for Divination

1. Cleansing Fossils

Before using fossils for divination, cleanse them to remove any residual energies:

- **Smoke Cleansing:** Pass the fossil through the smoke of sage, palo santo, or incense.
- **Earth Cleansing:** Bury the fossil in soil for 24 hours to recharge its grounding energy.
- **Moonlight Cleansing:** Leave the fossil under the light of the full moon to infuse it with intuitive energy.

2. Charging Fossils

After cleansing, charge your fossil with your intention:

- Hold the fossil in your hands and visualize it glowing with energy.
- Speak your intention aloud, such as:
  "I charge this fossil with the power to reveal insights into the past, present, and future."

Fossil Divination Methods

1. Fossil Casting

In this method, fossils are cast onto a cloth or into a shallow bowl, and their positions are interpreted.

Materials Needed:

- A collection of small fossils (e.g., ammonites, trilobites, or petrified wood pieces)
- A cloth or bowl with a marked circle or grid

Steps:

1. Hold the fossils in your hands and focus on your question or intention.
2. Toss the fossils onto the cloth or into the bowl. Observe their positions and relationships to each other.
3. Interpret the spread based on:
   - **Placement:** Fossils closer to the center represent immediate concerns, while those farther away reflect distant influences.
   - **Types of Fossils:** Use the symbolism of each fossil type to understand its message.
   - **Patterns:** Look for shapes or clusters that may hold additional meaning.

2. Fossil Scrying

Scrying involves gazing into the fossil to receive intuitive messages and visions.

Materials Needed:

- A single, polished fossil (ammonite or petrified wood works well)
- A darkened room or candlelit space

Steps:

1. Sit comfortably and hold the fossil at eye level. Focus on its texture, patterns, and details.
2. Ask your question silently or aloud.
3. Allow your mind to relax and notice any images, feelings, or thoughts that arise. These impressions are the fossil's way of communicating insights.
4. Record your impressions in a journal for further reflection.

3. Fossil Pendulum
This method uses a fossil as a pendulum to answer yes-or-no questions.
Materials Needed:

- A fossil pendulum or a small fossil tied to a string
- A pendulum chart or flat surface

Steps:

1. Hold the pendulum steady and ask it to show you its signals (e.g., swinging clockwise for "yes" and counterclockwise for "no").
2. Focus on your question and allow the pendulum to move naturally.
3. Interpret its motion to receive your answer.

4. Fossil Meditation
Meditate with a fossil to receive insights and guidance.
Materials Needed:

- A fossil that resonates with your intention
- A quiet space

Steps:

1. Hold the fossil in your hands and close your eyes.
2. Visualize yourself traveling back in time to when the fossil was formed. Imagine its environment and the life it once held.
3. Ask the fossil to share its wisdom, allowing impressions or messages to come through.
4. Write down any insights or feelings after the meditation.

Ritual for Fossil Divination

This ritual creates a sacred space for performing fossil divination, ensuring clear and accurate readings.

Materials Needed:

- A fossil or collection of fossils
- A white candle (for clarity)
- Incense (e.g., frankincense or sandalwood)
- A cloth or casting bowl

Steps:

1. Light the candle and incense to purify the space.
2. Place the fossil(s) on the cloth or in the bowl, holding them in your hands to connect with their energy.
3. Speak your intention aloud, such as:
   "Ancient relics, wise and old,
   Reveal the truths your stories hold.
   Past, present, future, let me see,
   Through your power, guide and teach me."
4. Perform your chosen divination method (casting, scrying, or pendulum) while focusing on your question.
5. Thank the fossil(s) for their guidance and record your insights in a journal.

Interpreting Fossil Readings

When interpreting fossil divinations, consider the following:

1. **Symbolism:** Reflect on the unique meaning of each fossil type.
2. **Positioning:** Observe how the fossils are arranged and their relationships to each other.
3. **Intuition:** Trust your instincts when interpreting patterns, impressions, or messages.

Using Fossil Divination for Specific Intentions

- **Past Exploration:** Use fossils to uncover how past events influence your present circumstances.
- **Present Guidance:** Seek clarity on current challenges or decisions.
- **Future Insights:** Gain perspective on potential outcomes and paths forward.

Incorporating Fossil Divination into Your Practice

1. **Daily Guidance:** Perform a simple casting or pendulum reading each morning to set your intentions for the day.
2. **Problem Solving:** Use fossil divination to gain insight into complex situations or choices.
3. **Spiritual Growth:** Meditate with fossils regularly to deepen your connection to their ancient wisdom.

The Legacy of Fossil Divination

Fossils are more than artifacts; they are timeless vessels of wisdom and power. Through fossil divination, you can connect to the Earth's history, align with its cycles, and uncover truths that guide you on your journey. This practice serves as a bridge between the prehistoric and the present, allowing you to channel ancient energy into your modern life.

Let the fossils guide you as you delve deeper into **The Dino Grimoire**, uncovering the secrets of the past to illuminate your future.

Chapter 14: Dinosaur Totems and Talismans

Throughout history, totems and talismans have been used to channel specific energies, enhance protection, and bring luck or guidance to their bearers. Dinosaur totems and talismans harness the primal power, unique symbolism, and ancient wisdom of these prehistoric creatures, making them potent tools in magickal practice. Each dinosaur species offers distinct qualities and energies, allowing you to craft personalized totems and talismans tailored to your intentions.

This chapter provides detailed guidance on selecting, crafting, and using dinosaur totems and talismans, as well as exploring the symbolic meanings of key dinosaur species.

Understanding Totems and Talismans

What Are Totems?

- **Totems** are symbolic representations of specific energies, often tied to an animal, plant, or element. In the context of dinosaurs, a totem represents the spirit and qualities of a particular species, acting as a guide and source of inspiration.

What Are Talismans?

- **Talismans** are objects imbued with energy or intention, designed to attract specific outcomes or provide protection. Dinosaur talismans can be crafted from fossils, bones, or representations of dinosaurs, charged with the energies of the species they symbolize.

Symbolism of Dinosaur Totems

Each dinosaur species carries distinct symbolism and energies. Choose a totem based on the traits or guidance you seek:

1. Tyrannosaurus Rex (T-Rex)

- **Symbolism:** Strength, dominance, leadership.
- **Energy:** Protection, courage, and the ability to overcome challenges.
- **Ideal for:** Gaining confidence, asserting authority, or standing your ground.

2. Triceratops

- **Symbolism:** Grounding, stability, and protection.
- **Energy:** Defensive energy and the ability to create safe boundaries.
- **Ideal for:** Protection, resilience, and nurturing relationships.

3. Velociraptor

- **Symbolism:** Intelligence, agility, and strategy.
- **Energy:** Quick thinking, adaptability, and precision.
- **Ideal for:** Success in decision-making, problem-solving, and competitive situations.

4. Stegosaurus

- **Symbolism:** Shielding, calmness, and resilience.
- **Energy:** Passive protection and emotional stability.
- **Ideal for:** Building spiritual shields and maintaining inner peace.

5. Brachiosaurus

- **Symbolism:** Growth, patience, and endurance.
- **Energy:** Nurturing and sustaining long-term projects.
- **Ideal for:** Manifesting goals and fostering patience.

6. Pterodactyl

- **Symbolism:** Freedom, perspective, and exploration.
- **Energy:** Soaring above challenges and gaining clarity.
- **Ideal for:** Vision quests, travel, and spiritual growth.

7. Ankylosaurus

- **Symbolism:** Defense, grounding, and persistence.
- **Energy:** Strong, impenetrable protection and resilience.
- **Ideal for:** Protection against negativity and persevering through adversity.

Crafting Dinosaur Totems and Talismans
Materials to Use

1. **Fossils or Fossil Replicas:** Ammonites, petrified wood, or small dinosaur bone fragments.
2. **Crystals and Stones:** Select stones that complement the energy of the dinosaur (e.g., obsidian for T-Rex, hematite for Triceratops).
3. **Wood or Clay:** Carve or mold dinosaur shapes or symbols for totems.
4. **Metal:** Create jewelry or keychains engraved with dinosaur designs.
5. **Feathers or Bones:** Incorporate symbolic elements connected to the dinosaur's environment.

Step-by-Step Guide to Crafting Totems
Materials Needed:

- A chosen fossil or symbolic item (e.g., small bone, crystal, or wood carving).
- Tools for carving or painting (optional).
- Candles in corresponding colors to the dinosaur's energy (e.g., red for T-Rex, green for Brachiosaurus).
- Incense or oils for cleansing (e.g., sage, cedarwood, or sandalwood).

Steps:

1. **Cleansing:** Cleanse the chosen item with smoke, moonlight, or salt to remove residual energies.
2. **Design and Decoration:** Carve or paint symbols associated with your chosen dinosaur onto the object, or leave it natural if it's a fossil.
3. **Charging the Totem:**
   - Light the candle in the dinosaur's corresponding color.
   - Hold the totem in your hands and focus on the energy you wish to channel.
   - Speak your intention aloud, such as:
     "[Dinosaur name], spirit of strength and might,
     Guide and protect me, day and night.
     With your power, I now align,
     Your ancient wisdom forever mine."
4. **Sealing the Energy:** Pass the totem through the candle flame (safely) or sprinkle it with water to seal the energy.

Step-by-Step Guide to Crafting Talismans
Materials Needed:

- A small fossil, crystal, or piece of jewelry.
- String, chain, or leather cord (if wearable).
- Herbs or oils that complement your intention.
- A pouch (if non-wearable).

Steps:

1. **Select Your Base:** Choose a fossil, crystal, or object that resonates with the dinosaur's energy.
2. **Add Enhancements:** Anoint the talisman with oils (e.g., rosemary for protection or lavender for peace) or include herbs in a pouch.
3. **Charge the Talisman:**
   - Hold the talisman and visualize it glowing with the energy of your chosen dinosaur.
   - Speak an affirmation, such as:
     "This talisman holds the power of the [Dinosaur name],
     A force of nature, ancient and wise.
     Guide my steps, protect my way,
     Empower me each and every day."
4. **Wear or Place:** Carry or wear the talisman to keep its energy close. For home protection, place it near entryways or under your pillow.

Using Totems and Talismans in Magickal Practices
1. Meditation

• Hold your totem or talisman during meditation to connect with the energy of the chosen dinosaur. Visualize its qualities infusing your mind and body.

2. Spellwork

• Place your totem or talisman on your altar during spells to amplify your intention. For example:
    ◦ Use a Stegosaurus totem in protection spells.
    ◦ Incorporate a Pterodactyl talisman in rituals for spiritual exploration.

3. Daily Wear

• Wear dinosaur talismans as jewelry to keep their energy with you throughout the day.

4. Home Protection

• Place a Triceratops totem near your front door to create a protective boundary.

Ritual to Activate Totems and Talismans
This activation ritual ensures that your totem or talisman is aligned with your energy and intention.
Materials Needed:

• A white candle (for purification)
• A green candle (for grounding)
• Incense (e.g., sandalwood or cedar)

Steps:

1. Light the white and green candles. Burn the incense to cleanse the space.
2. Hold the totem or talisman in your hands and close your eyes.
3. Visualize the chosen dinosaur appearing before you, infusing the object with its energy.
4. Speak aloud:
    "Spirit of the [Dinosaur name], I call to thee,
    Infuse this [totem/talisman] with your energy.

Strength and wisdom, fierce and true,
Guide my path in all I do."

5. Place the totem or talisman on your altar overnight to absorb the ritual's energy.

Caring for Dinosaur Totems and Talismans

1. **Regular Cleansing:** Cleanse your totems and talismans monthly or after intense use to maintain their potency.
2. **Recharging:** Place them under the full moon or on a bed of crystals to recharge their energy.
3. **Storage:** Keep your totems and talismans in a dedicated space when not in use, such as a pouch or altar.

The Legacy of Dinosaur Totems and Talismans

Dinosaur totems and talismans allow you to channel the wisdom and power of these ancient creatures, creating a bridge between their primal energy and your modern magickal practice. Whether used for guidance, protection, or empowerment, these tools offer a unique and personal way to connect with the timeless forces of the prehistoric world.

Let these ancient symbols guide and protect you as you delve deeper into **The Dino Grimoire**, unlocking the secrets of prehistoric magick in your life.

Chapter 15: Healing Magick of the Brachiosaurus

The Brachiosaurus, one of the most iconic dinosaurs of the Jurassic period, is a symbol of gentle strength, resilience, and nurturing energy. Its towering presence and herbivorous nature evoke a sense of calm, patience, and harmony, making it a perfect guide for healing magick. Whether you seek to heal physically, emotionally, or spiritually, the energy of the Brachiosaurus can provide steady support, encouraging growth and renewal.

This chapter explores the healing magick of the Brachiosaurus, offering rituals, meditations, and practical guidance for invoking its gentle yet powerful energy.

The Symbolism of the Brachiosaurus

The Brachiosaurus carries profound symbolic meaning that aligns perfectly with the principles of healing magick:

1. **Gentle Strength:** Despite its massive size, the Brachiosaurus was a peaceful herbivore, symbolizing strength through kindness and patience.
2. **Nurturing Energy:** Its long neck allowed it to reach high into the trees for sustenance, symbolizing the ability to nourish oneself and others.
3. **Growth and Renewal:** As a creature dependent on the Earth's vegetation, the Brachiosaurus is deeply connected to cycles of growth and regeneration.
4. **Endurance and Stability:** Its immense size and grounded nature reflect the stability and resilience needed for the healing process.

The Energetic Attributes of the Brachiosaurus

The energy of the Brachiosaurus is slow, steady, and deeply supportive. It resonates with the following qualities:

- **Earth Element:** Grounded, stable, and deeply connected to the healing energy of the planet.
- **Patience and Perseverance:** Healing, like the growth of a giant tree, takes time and commitment.
- **Nurturing Spirit:** The Brachiosaurus embodies care and nourishment, both for oneself and others.
- **Emotional Harmony:** Its peaceful nature can help calm turbulent emotions and restore balance.

Preparing to Work with Brachiosaurus Energy
1. Create a Healing Space
Design a space that reflects the nurturing energy of the Brachiosaurus:

- Use earthy tones like green, brown, and soft gold to create a calming atmosphere.
- Incorporate plants, trees, or images of forests to connect with its natural habitat.
- Place crystals like rose quartz, green aventurine, or moss agate on your altar for their healing properties.

2. Ground and Center Yourself
The Brachiosaurus's energy is deeply grounded. Begin by standing barefoot on the Earth (if possible) and visualizing roots growing from your feet into the ground. Feel yourself becoming stable and supported, like a tree deeply rooted in fertile soil.

3. Meditate on the Brachiosaurus
Visualize a Brachiosaurus moving gracefully through a prehistoric forest, its massive body radiating calm and gentle strength. Imagine its healing energy surrounding you, filling you with a sense of peace and renewal.

Rituals for Healing with the Brachiosaurus
1. Physical Healing Ritual: Strength Through Resilience
This ritual channels the strength and nurturing energy of the Brachiosaurus to support physical healing and recovery.
Materials Needed:

- A green candle (for healing and growth)
- A piece of moss agate or green aventurine
- A small plant or tree branch (real or symbolic)

Steps:

1. Light the green candle and place the moss agate or aventurine beside it.
2. Hold the plant or tree branch in your hands, visualizing it as a symbol of life and renewal.
3. Chant:
   "Brachiosaurus, steady and strong,
   Grant me healing all day long.
   Like the trees that reach the sky,
   Help my body renew and thrive."
4. Place the plant or branch near your bed or in a healing space as a reminder of the energy you've invoked. Keep the crystal with you during your recovery.

2. Emotional Healing Ritual: Calming the Storm
Use this ritual to call on the Brachiosaurus's peaceful energy to soothe emotional pain and restore balance.
Materials Needed:

- A blue candle (for emotional calm)
- A piece of rose quartz or amethyst
- A bowl of water

Steps:

1. Light the blue candle and place the bowl of water on your altar. Hold the rose quartz or amethyst in your hands.
2. Visualize the Brachiosaurus standing beside you, its gentle presence calming your emotions like still waters.
3. Say:
   "Brachiosaurus, gentle and wise,
   Bring me peace, let the pain subside.

Calm my heart, restore my soul,
Help me feel balanced, peaceful, and whole."

4. Dip your hands into the water, imagining it washing away your emotional pain. Let the candle burn for as long as feels right, then extinguish it with gratitude.

3. Spiritual Healing Ritual: Reaching for the Light

This ritual invokes the Brachiosaurus's ability to reach for sustenance as a metaphor for spiritual growth and healing.

Materials Needed:

- A gold or white candle (for spiritual renewal)
- A clear quartz crystal
- A tree or tall plant (real or symbolic)

Steps:

1. Light the candle and place the quartz on your altar. Stand or sit near the tree or plant.
2. Visualize yourself as the tree, reaching upward for light and nourishment. Imagine the Brachiosaurus guiding you, its energy encouraging your growth.
3. Chant:
   "Brachiosaurus, reaching high,
   Lift my spirit toward the sky.
   Help me heal, renew my soul,
   Guide me to become whole."
4. Hold the quartz as a talisman for spiritual growth and healing. Meditate with it regularly to maintain your connection.

Daily Practices to Strengthen Your Connection

1. **Carry a Symbol:** Keep a small fossil or crystal associated with the Brachiosaurus (like petrified wood) to remind you of its healing energy.
2. **Practice Grounding:** Spend time outdoors, connecting with trees and the Earth to align with the Brachiosaurus's grounded energy.
3. **Visualize Healing:** Each morning, visualize the Brachiosaurus surrounding you with a gentle glow of healing energy.

Using Brachiosaurus Energy in Specific Healing Work

1. Chronic Illness or Long-Term Recovery

The Brachiosaurus's slow, steady energy is ideal for supporting long-term healing. Perform the physical healing ritual regularly to maintain resilience.

2. Trauma and Emotional Wounds

The calm and nurturing presence of the Brachiosaurus can help soothe deep emotional scars. Use the emotional healing ritual to release pain and foster self-compassion.

3. Personal Growth and Renewal

The Brachiosaurus's connection to growth makes it an excellent guide for those seeking to rebuild their lives or embark on a spiritual journey.

Ritual to Charge a Healing Talisman

Create a healing talisman infused with the energy of the Brachiosaurus.

Materials Needed:

- A piece of green aventurine or moss agate
- A green or white candle
- A bowl of soil

Steps:

1. Light the candle and place the stone in the bowl of soil.
2. Visualize the Brachiosaurus standing tall, its energy flowing into the stone.
3. Chant:
   "Brachiosaurus, healer divine,
   Infuse this stone with power and time.
   Strength to heal, steady and pure,
   Grant this talisman the power to endure."
4. Carry the talisman with you or place it near your bed during recovery.

The Legacy of Brachiosaurus Healing Magick

The Brachiosaurus teaches us that healing is not an instant process but a journey of growth, patience, and self-nurturing. By aligning with its energy, you can find the strength to overcome physical, emotional, and spiritual wounds, becoming more balanced and whole.

Let the gentle yet powerful energy of the Brachiosaurus guide you as you delve deeper into **The Dino Grimoire**, unlocking the ancient secrets of healing and renewal.

Chapter 16: Dinosaur Bones in Spellcraft

Dinosaur bones and fossils are powerful tools in magickal practice, imbued with the timeless energy of the Earth and the ancient creatures that once roamed it. These remnants of prehistoric life hold immense spiritual significance, acting as conduits for grounding, transformation, protection, and ancient wisdom. By incorporating dinosaur bones and fossils into spellcraft, practitioners can access their primal power to enhance rituals, amplify intentions, and connect with the deep history of the Earth.

This chapter explores the practical applications of dinosaur bones and fossils in rituals and spellwork, offering detailed instructions on how to use these ancient tools effectively.

The Magickal Significance of Dinosaur Bones

Dinosaur bones, whether real fossils or symbolic representations, carry profound energy that can amplify magickal practices:

1. **Earth Element Energy:** Fossils are deeply connected to the Earth, making them ideal for grounding, stability, and protection.
2. **Ancient Wisdom:** The millions of years embedded in fossils resonate with timeless knowledge, making them powerful tools for divination and insight.
3. **Strength and Resilience:** The survival of these bones through eons symbolizes endurance and transformation, qualities that can be harnessed in spellwork.
4. **Primal Energy:** Dinosaur bones connect practitioners to the raw, untamed energy of the prehistoric world, ideal for spells involving personal power and courage.

Choosing Dinosaur Bones and Fossils for Magick

Different types of fossils and bones carry unique energies. Choose based on the intention of your spellwork:

Ammonites

- **Energy:** Cycles, transformation, and protection.
- **Uses:** Perfect for spells involving change, renewal, or shielding against negativity.

Petrified Wood

- **Energy:** Stability, grounding, and patience.
- **Uses:** Ideal for grounding rituals or manifesting long-term goals.

Dinosaur Bones or Fragments

- **Energy:** Strength, resilience, and primal power.
- **Uses:** Excellent for spells involving courage, endurance, or overcoming challenges.

Fossilized Teeth

- **Energy:** Sharpness, precision, and focus.
- **Uses:** Use in spells for decisiveness, problem-solving, or competitive situations.

Amber (Fossilized Resin)

- **Energy:** Preservation, protection, and solar energy.
- **Uses:** Ideal for healing, protective charms, and vitality spells.

Preparing Dinosaur Bones for Spellcraft

Before using dinosaur bones or fossils in magick, it's essential to cleanse and charge them to align with your intentions.

1. Cleansing

- **Smoke Cleansing:** Pass the fossil through the smoke of sage, cedar, or palo santo to remove residual energy.
- **Salt Cleansing:** Place the fossil in a bowl of sea salt overnight to purify it.
- **Earth Cleansing:** Bury the fossil in soil for 24 hours to reconnect it with the Earth's energy.

2. Charging

- Hold the fossil in your hands and visualize it glowing with energy. Speak your intention aloud, such as:
  "I charge this [bone/fossil] with the power of strength and resilience,
  Aligned with my purpose, pure and clear."

Rituals and Spells Using Dinosaur Bones
1. Grounding Ritual: Anchoring with Ancient Strength
This ritual uses dinosaur bones to ground your energy and connect deeply with the Earth.
Materials Needed:

- A piece of petrified wood or a bone fossil
- A bowl of soil
- A green candle

Steps:

1. Light the green candle and place the fossil in the bowl of soil.
2. Hold the bowl and visualize roots growing from your body into the Earth, anchoring you in its ancient energy.
3. Chant:
   "Bone of the Earth, steady and strong,
   Ground me where I belong.
   Anchor my soul, keep me whole,
   With your strength, make me bold."
4. Place the fossil on your altar or carry it with you to maintain this grounding energy.

2. Protection Spell: The Fossil Shield
This spell creates a protective barrier using the energy of dinosaur bones.
Materials Needed:

- A piece of ammonite or a fossilized bone
- A black candle
- A circle of salt or stones

Steps:

1. Light the black candle and place the fossil in the center of the circle.
2. Sit within the circle and visualize the fossil radiating a shield of protective energy around you.
3. Chant:
   "Bone of the ancient, shield me now,
   Guard my space, this I vow.
   No harm shall enter, no ill shall stay,
   Protected I am, come what may."
4. Keep the fossil near entryways or on your person as a protective talisman.

3. Strength Spell: Channeling Primal Power

This spell harnesses the resilience of dinosaur bones to boost personal strength and courage.

Materials Needed:

- A piece of dinosaur bone or fossilized tooth
- A red candle
- A piece of hematite

Steps:

1. Light the red candle and hold the fossil in one hand and the hematite in the other.
2. Visualize the dinosaur's strength flowing into you, filling you with courage and determination.
3. Chant:
   "Ancient power, fierce and true,
   Grant me strength in all I do.
   Like the bones that weather time,
   I am strong, my will divine."
4. Carry the hematite and fossil as talismans to maintain this energy.

4. Transformation Ritual: Fossil Phoenix

Use this ritual to let go of the old and embrace transformation, inspired by the fossilization process.

Materials Needed:

- A fossilized shell or ammonite
- A white and black candle
- A bowl of water

Steps:

1. Light the black candle and hold the fossil, focusing on what you wish to release.
2. Dip the fossil into the water and visualize it being cleansed of old energy.
3. Light the white candle and hold the fossil again, envisioning new energy filling the space left by what you released.
4. Chant:
   "From fossilized past to future bright,
   Transform my spirit with ancient might.
   Let old ways fade, let new ones grow,
   Through ancient wisdom, my path I'll know."
5. Keep the fossil on your altar as a symbol of your transformation.

Daily Practices with Dinosaur Bones

1. **Meditation Tool:** Hold a fossil during meditation to access its ancient energy and wisdom.
2. **Altar Decoration:** Place fossils on your altar to enhance its grounding and protective energy.
3. **Carry as Talismans:** Keep small fossils or bone fragments with you for daily strength and support.

Enhancing Spellcraft with Fossil Energy

- **Amplifying Intentions:** Use fossils to enhance the potency of spells by placing them on your altar or holding them during rituals.
- **Elemental Work:** Align fossils with the Earth element to ground and stabilize your magick.
- **Layered Magick:** Combine fossils with complementary crystals, herbs, or oils to create multi-layered spells.

Ritual to Dedicate Dinosaur Bones for Magick

This dedication ritual aligns dinosaur bones or fossils with your specific magickal purpose.

Materials Needed:

- A bone or fossil
- A white candle (for purity)
- A small bowl of salt water

Steps:

1. Light the white candle and hold the fossil above the bowl of salt water.
2. Speak your intention aloud, such as:
   "Ancient relic, wise and true,
   I dedicate your power to [intention].
   Guide my spells, protect my space,
   With your strength, my magick embrace."
3. Dip the fossil into the salt water to seal the dedication.
4. Place the fossil on your altar or carry it as a talisman.

The Legacy of Dinosaur Bones in Magick

Dinosaur bones and fossils connect us to the ancient past while empowering our present and future magickal practices. By incorporating these timeless tools into your spellwork, you can draw on their strength, wisdom, and resilience to create transformative results.

Let the enduring energy of dinosaur bones guide your magickal journey as you explore **The Dino Grimoire**, unlocking the secrets of prehistoric power and ancient wisdom.

Chapter 17: The Magick of Ancient Plants

Long before humans walked the Earth, prehistoric flora played a vital role in shaping ecosystems, providing nourishment, and creating the balance necessary for life. These ancient plants—ferns, cycads, ginkgo trees, horsetails, and conifers—carry the primal energy of resilience, transformation, and growth, making them powerful allies in magickal practice. Incorporating their symbolism, energy, and modern descendants into spellcraft can enhance rituals, foster grounding, and connect practitioners to the deep roots of the Earth's history.

This chapter explores the magickal properties of ancient plants and provides detailed guidance on how to use them in rituals, spells, and everyday magick.

The Importance of Prehistoric Flora in Magick

Ancient plants hold unique spiritual and magickal significance, drawn from their age, adaptability, and contribution to life on Earth:

1. **Resilience:** These plants survived cataclysmic changes and adapted to shifting environments, embodying strength and persistence.
2. **Cycle of Life:** As providers of oxygen and nourishment, prehistoric plants symbolize growth, renewal, and the interconnectedness of all life.
3. **Earth Element Energy:** Rooted in the Earth, these plants are ideal for grounding, stability, and fertility magick.
4. **Timeless Wisdom:** Their ancient origins connect practitioners to the primal energy of the planet, offering insight into life's deeper rhythms and cycles.

Key Prehistoric Plants and Their Magickal Properties

1. Ferns

- **Historical Background:** Among the oldest plants on Earth, ferns thrived in the Carboniferous period and remain largely unchanged today.
- **Magickal Properties:** Growth, resilience, protection, and luck.
- **Uses:** Ideal for spells involving new beginnings, fertility, or shielding against negativity.

2. Cycads

- **Historical Background:** Cycads are ancient seed plants that flourished during the Jurassic period.
- **Magickal Properties:** Stability, endurance, and prosperity.
- **Uses:** Use in rituals for financial growth or creating a stable foundation for long-term goals.

3. Ginkgo Trees

- **Historical Background:** The ginkgo tree, often called a "living fossil," dates back over 270 million years.
- **Magickal Properties:** Longevity, memory, and healing.
- **Uses:** Ideal for spells to enhance memory, support healing, or invoke ancient wisdom.

4. Horsetails

- **Historical Background:** Horsetails, thriving since the Devonian period, were among the dominant plants of prehistoric forests.
- **Magickal Properties:** Cleansing, renewal, and protection.
- **Uses:** Use in purification rituals or spells to release old energy and invite new growth.

5. Conifers (Pines, Cedars, and Junipers)

- **Historical Background:** Conifers have existed since the late Carboniferous period and are tied to many ancient ecosystems.
- **Magickal Properties:** Protection, prosperity, and spiritual elevation.
- **Uses:** Use pine needles for prosperity spells, cedar for cleansing, and juniper for protection rituals.

Modern Equivalents of Prehistoric Plants

Many prehistoric plants have modern counterparts that can be used in magickal practice:

- **Ferns:** Use common ferns for protection or growth spells.
- **Cycads:** Seek out ornamental cycads like sago palms for rituals involving prosperity or endurance.
- **Ginkgo Leaves:** Collect ginkgo leaves to enhance memory or connect with ancient wisdom.
- **Horsetails:** Harvest horsetails from natural areas for cleansing and renewal magick.
- **Pine, Cedar, and Juniper:** Collect needles, cones, or essential oils from these conifers to incorporate their energy.

Preparing Ancient Plants for Magickal Use
1. Harvesting with Intention

- Always ask permission from the plant before harvesting.
- Leave an offering, such as water, seeds, or a silent prayer of gratitude.
- Harvest only what you need and never take from endangered species.

2. Drying and Storing

- Dry leaves, needles, or stems in a cool, dark place to preserve their energy.
- Store in labeled jars or pouches, keeping them in a sacred or clean space.

3. Cleansing and Charging

- Cleanse plants by passing them through incense smoke or sprinkling them with salt water.
- Charge them by leaving them in sunlight, moonlight, or near a crystal grid aligned with their purpose.

Rituals and Spells Using Ancient Plants
1. Growth Spell: Flourishing Like a Fern
This spell uses ferns to promote personal growth and new beginnings.
Materials Needed:

- A fresh or dried fern frond
- A green candle
- A bowl of soil

Steps:

1. Light the green candle and place the fern on the soil.
2. Visualize yourself growing like a fern, resilient and abundant.
3. Chant:
   "Fern of old, green and bright,
   Help me grow, grant me light.
   Through change and time, I will thrive,
   Your energy keeps my dreams alive."
4. Place the soil in a garden or pot, and keep the fern nearby as a reminder of your intention.

2. Stability Ritual: Rooted Like a Cycad
This ritual channels the energy of cycads to create stability and endurance in your life.
Materials Needed:

- A sago palm frond or representation of a cycad
- A brown candle
- A small stone (e.g., petrified wood or hematite)

Steps:

1. Light the brown candle and hold the frond and stone in your hands.
2. Visualize roots growing from your feet into the Earth, grounding you in stability.
3. Chant:
   "Cycad ancient, rooted deep,
   Your strength and wisdom, I now keep.
   Steady and strong, I will remain,
   Through storms and trials, I sustain."
4. Keep the stone with you as a talisman of stability and strength.

3. Memory Spell: Wisdom of the Ginkgo

This spell uses ginkgo leaves to enhance memory and access ancient wisdom.

Materials Needed:

- A ginkgo leaf or extract
- A yellow candle
- A piece of clear quartz

Steps:

1. Light the yellow candle and place the ginkgo leaf and quartz in front of it.
2. Hold the quartz and visualize your mind opening like the ginkgo's fan-shaped leaves.
3. Chant:
   "Ginkgo tree, ancient and wise,
   Open my mind, clear my eyes.
   Memory sharp, knowledge flows,
   Through your wisdom, my spirit grows."
4. Carry the quartz with you when you need focus or clarity.

4. Cleansing Ritual: Horsetail Purification

This ritual uses horsetails to cleanse and renew your energy.

Materials Needed:

- A bundle of horsetail or representation of the plant
- A white candle
- A bowl of salt water

Steps:

1. Light the white candle and hold the horsetail bundle.
2. Pass the horsetail over your body, visualizing it sweeping away negativity.
3. Dip the horsetail in the salt water and chant:
   "Horsetail of old, cleanse and renew,
   Sweep away the old, bring forth the true.
   Through your strength, I find my way,
   Refreshed and clear, I greet the day."
4. Dispose of the salt water and horsetail respectfully to complete the ritual.

Incorporating Ancient Plants into Everyday Magick

1. **Plant Correspondences:** Use ancient plants in spells aligned with their properties, such as protection or growth.
2. **Herbal Teas:** Use safe ancient plant counterparts (like ginkgo) to brew teas for healing or focus.
3. **Decorating Sacred Spaces:** Add ferns, cycads, or conifer branches to your altar for grounding energy.

The Legacy of Prehistoric Plants in Magick

Prehistoric flora embodies resilience, growth, and the cycles of life. By incorporating their energies into your magickal practice, you connect to the ancient roots of the Earth and its timeless rhythms. Whether invoking protection, promoting growth, or seeking renewal, the magick of ancient plants serves as a powerful ally in your spiritual journey.

Let the wisdom and energy of these ancient allies guide your path as you delve deeper into **The Dino Grimoire**, unlocking the secrets of prehistoric magick and earthly connection.

Chapter 19: Awakening the Prehistoric Self

Deep within each of us lies a connection to the primal forces of the Earth, an ancient energy inherited from the long-forgotten ancestors who walked this planet before recorded history. Awakening the prehistoric self is about reconnecting with your primal instincts, unlocking the raw magick of survival, resilience, and intuition, and embracing the natural rhythms of life. By delving into this primordial energy, you can awaken your magickal ancestry and forge a deeper bond with the Earth's ancient power.

This chapter provides techniques, rituals, and practices to help you rediscover your prehistoric self, enabling you to channel this energy into your magickal and spiritual practices.

The Concept of the Prehistoric Self

The prehistoric self refers to the deeply embedded instincts and energies that link us to our distant ancestors and the primal forces that shaped early life. These instincts, often dulled by modern life, include:

1. **Survival Instincts:** The ability to sense danger, navigate challenges, and persevere.
2. **Primal Intuition:** The deep, unspoken understanding of nature and energy flows.
3. **Connection to Earth:** A profound bond with the planet, its rhythms, and its cycles.
4. **Ancestral Magick:** The spiritual practices, rituals, and wisdom of early humans who lived in harmony with the natural world.

Awakening the prehistoric self allows you to access this reservoir of knowledge and power, enriching your magickal practice and deepening your connection to the Earth.

Signs That Your Prehistoric Self Is Dormant

- Difficulty grounding or feeling disconnected from nature.
- Lack of trust in your intuition or inner voice.
- Feeling overwhelmed by modern life and its distractions.
- Struggles with personal resilience or navigating challenges.

By awakening your prehistoric self, you can reclaim these abilities and find balance, strength, and a sense of purpose.

Techniques for Reconnecting with Your Prehistoric Self
1. Grounding Through Earth Connection
Reconnecting with the Earth is the foundation of awakening your prehistoric self.
Practice:

1. Stand barefoot on natural ground (soil, grass, or sand) to create a physical connection with the Earth.
2. Close your eyes and visualize roots growing from your feet, sinking deep into the Earth.
3. Imagine drawing ancient energy up through these roots, filling your body with strength and stability.
4. Repeat the affirmation:
   "I am one with the Earth, grounded and strong.
   The ancient wisdom flows through me, where I belong."

2. Activate Primal Intuition
Your prehistoric self is deeply intuitive, capable of sensing energy shifts and recognizing patterns in nature.
Practice:

1. Spend time observing the natural world—watch how the wind moves, listen to birds, or follow the path of an animal.
2. Practice silent sitting in nature, focusing on your breath and allowing your senses to expand.
3. Reflect on moments when you've felt a "gut instinct" and how acting on it led to clarity.
4. Journal your observations to strengthen your intuitive awareness.

3. Ritual Dance of the Ancestors
Physical movement is a powerful way to awaken your prehistoric self, connecting you to the rhythms of life.
Practice:

1. Create a sacred space outdoors or in a quiet room.
2. Light a fire or a red candle to symbolize primal energy.
3. Play rhythmic drumming or natural sounds (or simply clap your hands and stomp your feet).
4. Close your eyes and let your body move freely, guided by instinct rather than thought. Imagine yourself as an early ancestor celebrating the Earth's cycles.
5. Chant:
   "Through the fire, through the land,
   I awaken, ancient and grand.
   Primal rhythm, beat of my soul,
   Reconnect me, make me whole."

4. Meditation with Fossils

Fossils hold the energy of ancient life, making them ideal tools for awakening your prehistoric self.

Practice:

1. Hold a fossil or place it on your altar.
2. Close your eyes and visualize yourself traveling back in time to the prehistoric Earth.
3. Imagine standing among dinosaurs, giant trees, and untouched landscapes, feeling the energy of this ancient world.
4. Ask the fossil to reveal the wisdom of the prehistoric self. Note any images, sensations, or messages that come to you.

Rituals for Awakening the Prehistoric Self

1. Primal Energy Activation Ritual

This ritual invokes the raw power of your prehistoric self to boost strength, resilience, and courage.

Materials Needed:

- A red or orange candle (for primal energy).
- A piece of petrified wood or bone fossil.
- A bowl of soil.

Steps:

1. Light the candle and hold the fossil in your hands.
2. Place the bowl of soil before you and dig your hands into it, feeling its texture and energy.
3. Chant:
   "From the Earth, my strength I claim,
   Primal power flows through my name.
   Resilient and bold, my spirit awakes,
   With ancient force, no fear shall take."
4. Hold the fossil to your heart and visualize your prehistoric self awakening within you.

2. Ancestral Connection Ceremony

Reconnect with the wisdom of your prehistoric ancestors through this ritual.

Materials Needed:

- A white candle (for ancestral connection).
- A bowl of water.
- A fossil or stone.

Steps:

1. Light the white candle and place the fossil in the bowl of water.
2. Close your eyes and visualize your ancestors gathering around you, their energy flowing into the fossil.
3. Chant:
   "Ancestors of Earth, ancient and wise,
   Share your knowledge, open my eyes.
   Through stone and water, your wisdom flows,
   Teach me the truths my spirit knows."
4. Meditate on any messages or impressions you receive.

Daily Practices for Strengthening the Prehistoric Self

1. **Morning Grounding Ritual:** Begin each day with a few minutes of barefoot grounding, visualizing prehistoric energy filling your body.
2. **Nature Walks:** Spend time outdoors, observing and attuning to the rhythms of nature.
3. **Instinct Exercises:** Practice making small decisions based on your intuition to build trust in your instincts.
4. **Sacred Fossil Carrying:** Keep a fossil or stone with you as a reminder of your connection to ancient Earth.

Magickal Benefits of Awakening the Prehistoric Self

- **Enhanced Intuition:** Deepen your ability to sense energy and make intuitive decisions.
- **Resilience and Strength:** Tap into primal energy to overcome challenges and stay grounded.
- **Connection to Nature:** Strengthen your bond with the Earth and its cycles.
- **Spiritual Insight:** Access ancient wisdom and integrate it into your magickal practice.

Awakening the Prehistoric Self in Modern Life

Incorporating the energy of your prehistoric self into daily life brings balance and purpose, helping you navigate the complexities of the modern world with primal strength and ancient wisdom. By reconnecting with your primal instincts and magickal ancestry, you can find clarity, empowerment, and a deeper understanding of your place within the Earth's cycles.

Let this journey into your prehistoric self guide your path as you explore **The Dino Grimoire**, embracing the timeless power of your ancient roots.

Chapter 20: The Velociraptor's Edge

The Velociraptor, with its speed, intelligence, and sharp precision, is one of the most iconic dinosaurs. Known for its agile movements and strategic prowess, the Velociraptor symbolizes quick thinking, adaptability, and calculated action. In magickal practice, channeling the energy of the Velociraptor allows practitioners to enhance speed, precision, and focus—qualities essential for success in fast-paced situations or when clarity and accuracy are required.

This chapter explores rituals, spells, and techniques to invoke the Velociraptor's edge, empowering you to act swiftly, make precise decisions, and maintain unwavering focus in your endeavors.

The Symbolism of the Velociraptor

The Velociraptor represents a unique combination of traits that make it a powerful magickal archetype:

1. **Speed:** Its agility and swiftness make it a symbol of quick action and decisiveness.
2. **Precision:** The Velociraptor's sharp claws and calculated movements embody accuracy and effectiveness.
3. **Intelligence:** As a strategic hunter, it symbolizes problem-solving, cunning, and adaptability.
4. **Focus:** Its ability to single-mindedly pursue its goals makes it an emblem of determination and discipline.

The Energetic Attributes of the Velociraptor

The Velociraptor's energy is dynamic and sharp, resonating with the following qualities:

- **Fire and Air Elements:** Its speed and precision combine the passion of fire with the clarity of air.
- **Keen Awareness:** The Velociraptor's heightened senses translate into enhanced perception and focus.
- **Strategic Action:** Its calculated approach to challenges makes it ideal for goal-oriented magick.

When to Invoke the Velociraptor's Edge

- When facing tight deadlines or high-pressure situations.
- To improve focus during study, work, or creative projects.
- To enhance precision in decision-making or physical activities.
- To overcome procrastination or mental fog.

Rituals for Enhancing Speed, Precision, and Focus
1. Swift Action Ritual: Harnessing Velociraptor Speed
This ritual channels the Velociraptor's energy to enhance quick thinking and efficient action.
Materials Needed:

- A red candle (for speed and vitality).
- A piece of carnelian or tiger's eye.
- A feather or symbolic object representing movement.

Steps:

1. Light the red candle and hold the carnelian or tiger's eye in your hand.
2. Visualize a Velociraptor sprinting swiftly and gracefully through its environment, its energy flowing into you.
3. Chant:
   "Velociraptor, swift and keen,
   Grant me speed, sharp and lean.
   Through your power, I now race,
   Quick and steady, I set my pace."
4. Carry the carnelian or tiger's eye as a talisman for speed and efficiency.

2. Precision Ritual: The Raptor's Claw
Use this ritual to sharpen your precision and accuracy, whether in physical actions, decisions, or creative endeavors.
Materials Needed:

- A white candle (for clarity and focus).
- A fossilized tooth, claw, or a small pointed crystal (e.g., quartz or obsidian).
- A piece of paper and pen.

Steps:

1. Light the white candle and hold the fossil or crystal in your dominant hand.
2. Write your intention or goal on the paper, focusing on being precise and clear.
3. Trace the paper with the fossil or crystal, visualizing its sharp energy carving out a path of precision.
4. Chant:
   "Velociraptor, sharp and true,
   Guide my hand in all I do.

With steady focus, let me see,
Precision clear, set me free."

5. Place the fossil or crystal on your altar and revisit the paper when you need a reminder of your goal.

3. Focus Enhancement Ritual: The Raptor's Gaze

This ritual aligns your mind with the Velociraptor's intense focus, allowing you to maintain concentration on tasks or goals.

Materials Needed:

- A yellow candle (for mental clarity).
- A piece of clear quartz.
- A mirror.

Steps:

1. Light the yellow candle and place the clear quartz in front of the mirror.
2. Look into the mirror, imagining yourself with the Velociraptor's keen, unwavering gaze.
3. Chant:
   "Velociraptor, sharp of mind,
   Help me focus, my thoughts aligned.
   Let distractions fade and fall,
   Laser focus, I hear your call."
4. Carry the quartz with you to maintain focus throughout the day.

4. Strategic Success Ritual: Mapping the Raptor's Path

Invoke the Velociraptor's intelligence and strategic energy to achieve success in complex situations.

Materials Needed:

- A green candle (for growth and success).
- A map or blank sheet of paper.
- A pen or marker.

Steps:

1. Light the green candle and place the map or paper on your altar.
2. Visualize a Velociraptor stalking its prey, calculating its moves with precision.
3. Use the pen to draw a symbolic path on the map or paper, representing the steps you need to take to achieve your goal.

4. Chant:

   "Velociraptor, wise and bright,
   Show me paths, clear my sight.
   Step by step, guide my way,
   Success is mine, come what may."

5. Keep the map or paper as a guide and reminder of your strategy.

Daily Practices to Strengthen the Velociraptor's Edge

1. **Meditative Visualization:** Spend a few minutes each morning visualizing the Velociraptor's swift and precise energy flowing into you.
2. **Carry a Raptor Talisman:** Wear or carry a small fossil, claw, or stone associated with speed and focus.
3. **Practice Quick Decisions:** Set small daily goals requiring quick and precise actions to strengthen your mental agility.
4. **Observe Movement in Nature:** Watch birds, animals, or natural phenomena to develop an appreciation for speed and precision in the natural world.

Ritual to Charge a Velociraptor Talisman
Create and charge a talisman to keep the Velociraptor's energy with you at all times.
Materials Needed:

- A small fossil, claw replica, or pointed crystal.
- A red, yellow, or white candle (for speed, focus, or precision).
- Incense (e.g., sandalwood or rosemary).

Steps:

1. Light the candle and incense, placing the talisman in front of you.
2. Hold your hands over the talisman and visualize the Velociraptor's energy infusing it.
3. Speak your intention aloud, such as:
   "Velociraptor, agile and bright,
   Infuse this talisman with your might.
   Speed and focus, sharp and true,
   Grant me strength in all I do."
4. Carry or wear the talisman to access the Velociraptor's energy throughout the day.

The Legacy of the Velociraptor in Magick
The Velociraptor's edge teaches us the value of quick thinking, precise action, and unwavering focus. By incorporating its energy into your magickal practice, you can navigate challenges with confidence, achieve your goals efficiently, and sharpen your instincts for success.

Let the Velociraptor's dynamic spirit guide you as you explore **The Dino Grimoire**, unlocking your potential to act with speed, precision, and clarity in all aspects of life.

Chapter 21: Dinosaur Dreams and Visions

Dreams and visions have long been considered gateways to the subconscious, the spiritual realm, and the collective memory of the Earth. Working with dinosaur energies in these altered states of consciousness can unlock profound insights, connect you to ancient wisdom, and reveal hidden truths about yourself and the world around you. Dinosaur dreamwork and vision quests tap into the primal energies of prehistoric times, providing guidance, empowerment, and a deeper connection to the Earth's ancient past.

This chapter explores the techniques, rituals, and interpretations for working with dinosaur energies in dreams and vision quests, offering practical ways to access this unique magickal realm.

The Power of Dinosaur Energies in Dreamwork and Vision Quests

Dinosaurs carry the primal energy of Earth's distant past, making them ideal guides for exploring deep, ancient layers of the psyche. Their energy in dreams and visions symbolizes:

1. **Transformation:** Dinosaurs represent the cycles of life, death, and rebirth, offering insights into personal evolution.
2. **Strength and Power:** Their presence in dreams can awaken inner strength and resilience.
3. **Wisdom of the Earth:** As creatures of the prehistoric world, dinosaurs carry the energy of ancient knowledge and natural rhythms.
4. **Connection to Ancestry:** Working with dinosaurs in dreams can bridge the gap between the modern self and primal instincts, connecting you to magickal ancestry.

Techniques for Dinosaur Dreamwork

1. Preparing for Dinosaur Dreams

Set the intention to connect with dinosaur energies before you sleep.

Steps:

1. **Create a Sacred Sleep Space:** Cleanse your bedroom with smoke, sound, or visualization to make it conducive to dreamwork.
2. **Choose a Focus Fossil or Crystal:** Place a dinosaur fossil or a crystal like amethyst (for dream clarity) or petrified wood (for grounding) under your pillow or on your bedside table.
3. **Set an Intention:** Before sleeping, speak aloud or write down your intention, such as:
   "I invite the energy of the dinosaurs to guide me in my dreams, revealing wisdom, strength, and insight."

2. Lucid Dreaming with Dinosaur Energy

Lucid dreaming allows you to consciously interact with the dinosaur energies that appear in your dreams.

Practice:

1. **Reality Checks:** Throughout the day, ask yourself, "Am I dreaming?" and look for unusual details. This habit increases your chances of becoming lucid in a dream.
2. **Dream Signs:** Pay attention to recurring symbols or themes, such as prehistoric landscapes or dinosaur imagery. Use these as cues for lucidity.
3. **Engage the Dinosaur:** Once lucid, approach any dinosaur in your dream and ask it questions, such as:
   - "What message do you have for me?"
   - "How can I harness your energy in my waking life?"

3. Dream Journaling

Keep a dream journal to record details of your dinosaur dreams. This helps you uncover patterns, messages, and themes over time.

Key Elements to Note:

- The type of dinosaur and its behavior.
- The environment (e.g., lush jungle, arid plains).
- Your emotions and actions within the dream.
- Any symbols or messages conveyed by the dinosaur.

Rituals for Dinosaur Dreamwork
1. Dream Invocation Ritual
This ritual invites dinosaur energy into your dreams for guidance and clarity.
Materials Needed:

- A fossil (e.g., ammonite, petrified wood, or bone fragment).
- A blue or purple candle (for dreams and intuition).
- Lavender or mugwort incense.

Steps:

1. Light the candle and incense, placing the fossil before you.
2. Hold the fossil and close your eyes, visualizing a prehistoric landscape with dinosaurs roaming peacefully.
3. Chant:
   "Guardians of time, ancient and wise,
   Enter my dreams, open my eyes.
   Teach me your secrets, guide my way,
   Through dream's portal, show me the day."
4. Place the fossil under your pillow or beside your bed, and go to sleep with the intention of dreaming about dinosaur energy.

2. Dinosaur Spirit Ally Ritual
This ritual helps you meet a specific dinosaur spirit guide in your dreams.
Materials Needed:

- A piece of clear quartz (for clarity).
- A green candle (for connection to nature).
- A small bowl of water.

Steps:

1. Light the green candle and place the quartz in the bowl of water.
2. Sit in meditation, focusing on your breath and the shimmering surface of the water.
3. Speak aloud:
   "Ancient spirits of the Earth,
   Guide my dreams, reveal your worth.
   Show me the one who walks my path,
   With wisdom to share and ancient craft."
4. Before sleeping, visualize the dinosaur spirit guide you wish to meet, inviting them to join your dream.

Vision Quests with Dinosaur Energy

Vision quests are intentional journeys into altered states of consciousness to seek guidance or insight. Dinosaur energy can be a powerful ally during these quests, offering strength, resilience, and ancient wisdom.

1. Preparing for a Vision Quest

- Choose a quiet, safe space, ideally outdoors in a natural setting.
- Gather grounding tools such as fossils, stones, or a drum for rhythmic sound.
- Set a clear intention for your quest, such as uncovering personal power, seeking guidance, or connecting to ancestral energy.

2. Vision Quest Practice
Materials Needed:

- A fossil or symbolic item.
- A drum or soft rhythmic music (optional).
- A journal for recording insights.

Steps:

1. Sit or lie comfortably, holding the fossil or symbolic item in your hand.
2. Close your eyes and visualize yourself stepping into a prehistoric world, surrounded by ancient landscapes and dinosaurs.
3. Allow a dinosaur to approach you and observe its behavior. Engage with it by asking questions or following where it leads.
4. When you feel ready, slowly return to your normal state of consciousness, grounding yourself by touching the Earth or holding a grounding stone.
5. Record your experience in your journal, noting any insights or messages.

Interpreting Dinosaur Dreams and Visions

The type of dinosaur and its actions in your dream or vision can provide clues to its message:

- **Tyrannosaurus Rex:** Represents strength, power, and leadership. It may challenge you to step into your authority or confront fears.
- **Triceratops:** Symbolizes protection and grounding, offering guidance on creating boundaries or stabilizing your life.
- **Velociraptor:** Highlights agility, precision, and quick thinking. It may advise you to act decisively or adapt to changing circumstances.
- **Brachiosaurus:** Represents growth, patience, and nurturing. It encourages long-term planning and emotional healing.
- **Pterodactyl:** Symbolizes freedom, perspective, and spiritual elevation. It may guide you to rise above challenges and see the bigger picture.

Daily Practices for Dinosaur Dreamwork

1. **Evening Reflection:** Spend a few moments each night reflecting on your dreams and setting intentions for the next.
2. **Fossil Meditation:** Hold a fossil during meditation to strengthen your connection to dinosaur energy before sleep.
3. **Visualization Exercise:** Imagine prehistoric landscapes and dinosaurs as you fall asleep, inviting their energy into your dreams.

Magickal Benefits of Dinosaur Dreamwork and Visions

- **Deeper Insights:** Gain clarity on personal challenges and spiritual questions.
- **Strength and Resilience:** Connect with the primal power of dinosaurs to build inner strength.
- **Guidance and Support:** Receive messages from dinosaur spirit allies that align with your life's path.
- **Connection to Ancestry:** Tap into ancient wisdom and instincts that guide your magickal practice.

Embracing Dinosaur Dreams and Visions in Magick

By working with dinosaur energies in dreams and vision quests, you can unlock a profound connection to the Earth's ancient past and the wisdom it holds. These experiences provide insight, empowerment, and a deeper understanding of your magickal path.

Let the dinosaurs guide your subconscious and spiritual journey as you explore **The Dino Grimoire**, uncovering the mysteries and magick of the prehistoric world.

Chapter 22: Fossil Grids for Energy Amplification

Fossil grids are powerful tools that utilize the ancient energy stored in fossils to amplify intentions and enhance the flow of magickal energy. Just as crystal grids align and focus energy through specific layouts, fossil grids harness the primal power of prehistoric life to create a strong connection to Earth's ancient forces. Fossils carry the wisdom, strength, and resilience of millions of years, making them potent allies for protection, healing, manifestation, and grounding.

This chapter provides a comprehensive guide to creating fossil grids, detailing their purpose, construction, and specific layouts for various magickal intentions.

The Magickal Power of Fossil Grids

Fossils are imbued with the energy of the Earth's history and the life that once thrived on it. Incorporating them into energy grids offers several benefits:

1. **Grounding Energy:** Fossils anchor the energy of the grid, creating a stable foundation for magickal work.
2. **Amplification:** The age and resilience of fossils amplify intentions, allowing for powerful energy flow.
3. **Ancient Wisdom:** Fossils connect the practitioner to Earth's ancient cycles, enhancing spiritual insight and awareness.
4. **Protection and Stability:** The fossilized remnants of prehistoric creatures provide energetic shielding and a sense of security.

Choosing Fossils for Energy Grids

Different fossils carry unique energies that can be harnessed for specific purposes. Choose fossils that align with your intention:

1. Ammonites

- **Energy:** Transformation, protection, and balance.
- **Best For:** Manifestation, protection grids, and emotional harmony.

2. Petrified Wood

- **Energy:** Stability, grounding, and patience.
- **Best For:** Healing, grounding grids, and long-term goal setting.

3. Dinosaur Bones

- **Energy:** Strength, resilience, and primal power.
- **Best For:** Protection, courage, and energy renewal.

4. Fossilized Coral

- **Energy:** Emotional healing, connection, and nurturing.
- **Best For:** Healing, emotional balance, and relationship grids.

5. Fossilized Teeth or Claws

- **Energy:** Precision, focus, and decisiveness.
- **Best For:** Success, clarity, and strategic action grids.

6. Amber (Fossilized Resin)

- **Energy:** Preservation, protection, and vitality.
- **Best For:** Cleansing, protective grids, and energizing intentions.

Designing a Fossil Grid

The design of your fossil grid determines how the energy flows and focuses. Consider these elements when creating your grid:

1. Shape of the Grid

- **Circle:** For protection, unity, and wholeness.
- **Triangle:** For manifestation, power, and direction.
- **Square:** For grounding, stability, and balance.
- **Spiral:** For transformation, growth, and evolution.

2. Placement of Fossils

- **Center Fossil (Anchor):** The most significant fossil representing the core intention.
- **Supporting Fossils:** Surrounding fossils that direct and amplify energy toward the center or outward.

3. Amplifiers

- Include crystals, stones, or additional fossils to enhance the grid's energy. Examples include quartz (amplification), obsidian (protection), or green aventurine (healing).

Creating a Fossil Grid: Step-by-Step
Materials Needed

- Fossils aligned with your intention.
- A flat surface or cloth to arrange the grid.
- Optional: Crystals, stones, or symbolic items for additional energy.
- A written intention or affirmation (optional).

Steps

1. **Set Your Intention**
   Clearly define the purpose of your fossil grid. Write it down if it helps focus your energy.
2. **Cleanse and Charge Your Fossils**
   Cleanse the fossils with smoke, salt water, or moonlight to remove residual energies. Charge them with your intention by holding each fossil and visualizing your desired outcome.
3. **Prepare the Space**
   Choose a quiet, sacred space for your grid. Cleanse the area to ensure a positive energy flow.
4. **Select a Layout**
   Choose a shape that aligns with your intention and arrange your fossils accordingly. Place the anchor fossil at the center.
5. **Activate the Grid**
   Once the fossils are arranged, activate the grid by pointing a wand, crystal, or your finger at the center fossil. Visualize energy connecting each fossil, creating a network of light.
6. **Focus Your Intention**
   Sit with the grid, meditate on your intention, and repeat an affirmation or chant related to your goal.
7. **Maintain the Grid**
   Keep the grid in place as long as needed. Cleanse and recharge it periodically to maintain its potency.

Fossil Grid Layouts for Specific Intentions
1. Protection Grid
Purpose: Create a shield against negative energies.
Layout:

- **Center Fossil:** Ammonite (for protective energy).
- **Supporting Fossils:** Dinosaur bones in a circle around the center.
- **Amplifiers:** Black tourmaline or obsidian at the four cardinal points.

Affirmation:
"Shield me with ancient strength and light,
Guard my spirit day and night."
2. Healing Grid
Purpose: Promote physical, emotional, or spiritual healing.
Layout:

- **Center Fossil:** Petrified wood (for grounding and renewal).
- **Supporting Fossils:** Fossilized coral arranged in a hexagonal pattern.
- **Amplifiers:** Rose quartz (for emotional healing) and green aventurine (for physical healing).

Affirmation:
"With ancient power, I now renew,
Healing light flows pure and true."
3. Manifestation Grid
Purpose: Attract abundance, success, or a specific goal.
Layout:

- **Center Fossil:** Ammonite (for transformation and balance).
- **Supporting Fossils:** Fossilized teeth or claws in a triangular layout pointing outward.
- **Amplifiers:** Citrine (for success) and pyrite (for abundance).

Affirmation:
"From ancient strength, my dreams take flight,
Manifesting goals with primal might."

4. Grounding Grid

Purpose: Provide stability and connect to Earth's energy.

Layout:

- **Center Fossil:** Petrified wood (for grounding).
- **Supporting Fossils:** Dinosaur bones arranged in a square pattern.
- **Amplifiers:** Hematite or smoky quartz at the corners for stability.

Affirmation:

"Root me deep, strong and sure,
Earth's ancient wisdom will endure."

5. Emotional Balance Grid

Purpose: Cultivate peace, harmony, and emotional resilience.

Layout:

- **Center Fossil:** Fossilized coral (for emotional healing).
- **Supporting Fossils:** Amber in a circular pattern.
- **Amplifiers:** Blue lace agate (for calm) and selenite (for harmony).

Affirmation:

"Peaceful flow, balance restored,
Emotional harmony, forever adored."

Maintaining and Evolving Your Fossil Grid

1. **Regular Cleansing:** Cleanse the fossils and space periodically to remove stagnant energy.
2. **Recharging:** Leave the fossils under moonlight or sunlight to recharge their energy.
3. **Adapting the Grid:** Modify the layout or fossils as your intention evolves.
4. **Integration:** Meditate near the grid or incorporate it into daily rituals to strengthen its energy.

Magickal Benefits of Fossil Grids

- **Amplified Intentions:** Fossil grids enhance the focus and power of your magickal work.
- **Connection to Ancient Energy:** They bridge the gap between the present and Earth's prehistoric past.
- **Grounding and Protection:** Fossil grids provide stability and shielding during transformative times.
- **Versatility:** They can be adapted for nearly any magickal purpose, from healing to manifestation.

The Legacy of Fossil Grids in Magick

Fossil grids combine the wisdom of prehistoric life with the focused energy of modern magickal practice. By incorporating fossils into energy grids, you can tap into the Earth's ancient power to manifest intentions, heal, and protect.

Let these grids be a reminder of your connection to the Earth's enduring strength as you explore **The Dino Grimoire**, uncovering the timeless magick of fossils and prehistoric energies.

Chapter 23: Prehistoric Lunar Magick

The Moon, with its ever-changing phases and gravitational pull, has been a guiding force on Earth since the dawn of time. In the prehistoric world, the Moon influenced tides, migration patterns, reproduction cycles, and the behaviors of ancient creatures. These same lunar energies are accessible to us today, allowing practitioners to align their magickal practices with the Moon's rhythms to enhance power, focus, and intention.

This chapter explores the connection between the Moon and the prehistoric world, delves into the significance of lunar phases in magick, and provides rituals and techniques to harness the Moon's energy for your magickal workings.

The Moon's Role in the Prehistoric World

In prehistoric times, the Moon was a dominant force that shaped the lives of ancient creatures and ecosystems. Its magickal significance is rooted in its influence on the natural world:

1. **Tides and Water Cycles:** The Moon's gravitational pull created tides, shaping the prehistoric coastlines and influencing the behaviors of marine creatures like ammonites and plesiosaurs.
2. **Reproduction and Fertility:** Many prehistoric species synchronized their reproductive cycles with the Moon, using its phases as a natural timer.
3. **Navigation:** Flying creatures such as pterosaurs may have used the Moon's light to navigate during nighttime flights.
4. **Cycles of Growth:** The Moon's phases mirrored the cycles of life, death, and rebirth, reflecting the natural rhythms of prehistoric Earth.

Understanding these connections allows us to align with the Moon's ancient energy and integrate it into modern magickal practices.

The Magickal Significance of Lunar Phases

Each phase of the Moon carries specific energies that influence magickal workings. By aligning your intentions with the Moon's phases, you can amplify the power of your rituals and spells:

1. New Moon

- **Energy:** Beginnings, introspection, planting seeds.
- **Magickal Work:** Set intentions, start new projects, and focus on self-reflection.
- **Prehistoric Connection:** Symbolizes the emergence of life from darkness, akin to the hatching of dinosaur eggs.

2. Waxing Crescent Moon

- **Energy:** Growth, expansion, and manifestation.
- **Magickal Work:** Build momentum toward goals, attract abundance, and focus on progress.
- **Prehistoric Connection:** Represents the nurturing energy of ferns and cycads growing during the lush prehistoric eras.

3. First Quarter Moon

- **Energy:** Action, decision-making, and overcoming obstacles.
- **Magickal Work:** Take decisive steps toward goals, break through challenges, and focus on strength.
- **Prehistoric Connection:** Embodies the strength and determination of dinosaurs like Triceratops pushing forward through adversity.

4. Waxing Gibbous Moon

- **Energy:** Refinement, preparation, and anticipation.
- **Magickal Work:** Fine-tune intentions, clarify goals, and amplify power.
- **Prehistoric Connection:** Reflects the nearing culmination of a process, much like the slow formation of fossils.

5. Full Moon

- **Energy:** Culmination, manifestation, and celebration.
- **Magickal Work:** Perform powerful rituals, release what no longer serves you, and harness peak energy.
- **Prehistoric Connection:** Mirrors the full bloom of prehistoric forests and the height of ecosystems' vibrancy.

6. Waning Gibbous Moon

- **Energy:** Gratitude, reflection, and sharing wisdom.
- **Magickal Work:** Reflect on lessons, give thanks, and release excess energy.
- **Prehistoric Connection:** Represents the cycles of decay and renewal in ancient ecosystems.

7. Last Quarter Moon

- **Energy:** Release, banishing, and letting go.
- **Magickal Work:** Break unhealthy patterns, banish negativity, and focus on endings.
- **Prehistoric Connection:** Reflects the extinction of species and the clearing of old to make way for the new.

8. Waning Crescent Moon

- **Energy:** Rest, introspection, and surrender.
- **Magickal Work:** Focus on healing, recuperation, and preparing for new beginnings.
- **Prehistoric Connection:** Symbolizes the quiet stillness before the dawn of new life.

Prehistoric Lunar Magick Rituals
1. New Moon Ritual: Planting Seeds of Intention
Purpose: Set intentions for growth and new beginnings.
Materials Needed:

- A fossilized seed or petrified wood (symbolizing growth).
- A black candle.
- A small pot of soil.

Steps:

1. Light the black candle and hold the fossilized seed or petrified wood.
2. Visualize the darkness of the New Moon as fertile ground for your intentions.
3. Speak your intention aloud, saying:
   "In the darkness, seeds are sown,
   With lunar power, let them grow."
4. Plant the fossil in the pot of soil as a symbolic gesture. Keep it on your altar during the lunar cycle.

2. Full Moon Ritual: Harnessing Peak Energy
Purpose: Amplify energy for manifestation or celebration.
Materials Needed:

- A dinosaur bone or tooth fossil (symbolizing strength).
- A white candle.
- A bowl of water.

Steps:

1. Light the white candle and place the fossil in the bowl of water.
2. Take the bowl outside or near a window to bathe in the Full Moon's light.
3. Chant:
   "Moon at its height, shining bright,
   Grant me power through this night.
   Ancient strength, bold and true,
   Manifest my will, as I ask of you."
4. Meditate on your intention and allow the Moon's energy to fill you.

3. Waning Moon Ritual: Releasing the Old
Purpose: Let go of negative energy or habits.
Materials Needed:

- A piece of amber (fossilized resin, for preservation and release).
- A black candle.
- A piece of paper and pen.

Steps:

1. Write down what you wish to release on the paper.
2. Light the black candle and hold the amber, focusing on its energy absorbing and transforming negativity.
3. Burn the paper in a fire-safe bowl, chanting:
   "As the Moon wanes, I release,
   All that hinders my inner peace.
   Amber's glow, cleanse and renew,
   With lunar power, I start anew."
4. Bury the ashes in the Earth as a symbol of letting go.

Daily Practices for Prehistoric Lunar Magick

1. **Lunar Observation:** Track the Moon's phases and journal how its energy influences you.
2. **Moonlit Meditation:** Spend time outdoors under the Moon's light, connecting to its energy.
3. **Dreamwork:** Place a fossil under your pillow to enhance lunar dreamwork during specific phases.

Magickal Correspondences for Lunar Phases

Phase	Element	Color	Fossil Type	Intention
New Moon	Earth	Black	Petrified Wood	Beginnings, planting seeds
Waxing Crescent	Air	Green	Ammonite	Growth, manifestation
First Quarter	Fire	Red	Dinosaur Bone	Action, overcoming obstacles
Waxing Gibbous	Water	Blue	Fossilized Coral	Refinement, preparation
Full Moon	Spirit	White	Fossilized Tooth	Culmination, celebration
Waning Gibbous	Water	Silver	Amber	Reflection, gratitude
Last Quarter	Fire	Gray	Ammonite	Release, banishing
Waning Crescent	Earth	Purple	Petrified Wood	Healing, rest

Aligning Your Magick with Prehistoric Lunar Energy

Incorporating prehistoric themes into your lunar magick strengthens your connection to the Earth's ancient cycles. Consider the following practices:

- **Dinosaur Spirit Guides:** Meditate with dinosaur energy during specific lunar phases to align with their unique strengths.
- **Lunar Fossil Talismans:** Carry fossils charged under different Moon phases to maintain their energy throughout the month.
- **Prehistoric Landscapes:** Visualize ancient environments during lunar rituals to deepen your connection to the Earth's past.

Magickal Benefits of Prehistoric Lunar Magick

- **Enhanced Intuition:** Aligning with lunar phases sharpens your inner awareness.
- **Empowered Intentions:** Working with the Moon's energy amplifies the potency of your spells.
- **Connection to Cycles:** Prehistoric lunar magick fosters a deeper understanding of nature's rhythms.
- **Healing and Renewal:** The Moon's phases provide opportunities for growth, reflection, and release.

The Legacy of Lunar Magick

The Moon has influenced life on Earth since its earliest days, shaping tides, ecosystems, and behaviors. By incorporating lunar phases into your magickal practice, you can honor its ancient power while aligning with its cycles to achieve balance, growth, and transformation.

Let the Moon guide your path as you explore **The Dino Grimoire**, connecting to the timeless rhythms of the prehistoric world and its magickal energies.

Chapter 24: Crafting a Prehistoric Altar

An altar is the heart of any magickal practice, serving as a sacred space to focus energy, perform rituals, and connect with spiritual forces. A prehistoric altar is a unique creation, designed to honor the ancient energies of the Earth, celebrate the power of fossils, and immerse the practitioner in the raw, primal magick of prehistoric times. By incorporating fossils, symbols, and sacred objects, a prehistoric altar becomes a powerful focal point for rituals, meditations, and daily magickal work.

This chapter provides detailed guidance on crafting and maintaining a prehistoric altar, including essential components, symbolic items, and ideas for personalized touches.

The Purpose of a Prehistoric Altar

A prehistoric altar serves as a connection point between the practitioner and the Earth's ancient past. Its purposes include:

1. **Honoring Ancient Energies:** Pay tribute to the power and wisdom of prehistoric life.
2. **Amplifying Magickal Intentions:** Use fossils and other objects to channel and focus energy.
3. **Creating a Sacred Space:** Establish a dedicated area for rituals, meditations, and spellcraft.
4. **Grounding Your Practice:** Anchor your magick in the primal energy of the Earth.

Choosing the Location for Your Prehistoric Altar

When selecting a location for your altar, consider the following:

1. **Quiet and Sacred Space:** Choose a place where you can work undisturbed, whether indoors or outdoors.
2. **Natural Light:** If possible, place your altar near a window or outside to connect with natural cycles.
3. **Connection to Earth:** Outdoor altars can incorporate soil, stones, and plants for added grounding energy.

Essential Components of a Prehistoric Altar

A prehistoric altar incorporates fossils, natural elements, and symbolic objects. Here are key components to include:

1. Fossils

Fossils are the foundation of a prehistoric altar, representing ancient energy and Earth's history. Choose fossils that resonate with your intentions:

- **Ammonites:** For transformation and protection.
- **Petrified Wood:** For grounding and stability.
- **Dinosaur Bones:** For strength and resilience.
- **Amber (Fossilized Resin):** For preservation and vitality.

Arrange these fossils prominently on your altar to serve as focal points for your practice.

2. Stones and Crystals

Complement the fossils with crystals and stones that enhance their energy. Examples include:

- **Quartz:** Amplifies energy and intentions.
- **Obsidian:** Provides protection and grounding.
- **Green Aventurine:** Supports growth and healing.
- **Citrine:** Encourages manifestation and success.

3. Candles

Candles represent the element of fire and bring warmth and focus to your altar. Use colors that align with your intentions:

- **Red:** For strength and action.
- **Green:** For growth and renewal.
- **White:** For purification and clarity.
- **Black:** For protection and banishing.

4. Natural Elements

Incorporate natural materials to ground your altar in Earth's energy:

- **Soil:** Symbolizes the nurturing Earth.
- **Plants:** Include ferns, cycads, or moss to represent prehistoric flora.
- **Water:** Use a bowl of water to reflect the ancient seas.
- **Feathers or Bones:** Symbolize prehistoric animals and their connection to life cycles.

5. Symbols of Prehistoric Life

Enhance the altar with symbolic representations of prehistoric creatures or themes:

- **Dinosaur Figurines:** Represent specific energies, such as the strength of the T-Rex or the agility of the Velociraptor.
- **Fossil Imprints:** Display fossilized footprints or plant impressions.
- **Artwork or Carvings:** Depicting prehistoric landscapes or creatures.

Designing Your Prehistoric Altar

The layout and design of your altar should reflect your intentions and personal connection to prehistoric magick. Here are some ideas:

1. Central Focus

Place a significant fossil or symbolic object at the center of your altar as the primary focal point. This could be a large ammonite, a dinosaur bone, or a petrified wood piece.

2. Elemental Representation

Arrange objects on your altar to represent the four elements:

- **Earth:** Fossils, stones, and soil.
- **Water:** A bowl of water or shell fossils.
- **Fire:** Candles or amber.
- **Air:** Feathers or incense.

3. Thematic Layers

Organize your altar in layers or sections that correspond to different aspects of prehistoric life:

- **Ancient Creatures:** Dinosaur bones, teeth, or figurines.
- **Prehistoric Plants:** Fossilized wood, fern leaves, or cycads.
- **Earth's History:** Rocks, soil, and fossils that represent different geological eras.

4. Sacred Geometry

Arrange your altar items in geometric patterns, such as circles, triangles, or spirals, to direct and amplify energy.

Personalizing Your Prehistoric Altar

Make your altar uniquely yours by incorporating items that resonate with your personal practice:

1. **Intentional Objects:** Include items that represent your goals or intentions, such as written affirmations, vision boards, or talismans.
2. **Seasonal Decor:** Update your altar with items that reflect the seasons, such as fresh flowers in spring or pine cones in winter.
3. **Prehistoric Themes:** Add creative touches, such as painted rocks, carved wood, or hand-drawn dinosaur symbols.

Rituals and Practices for Your Prehistoric Altar

Once your altar is set up, use it for various magickal practices:

1. Morning Grounding Ritual

Begin each day by grounding yourself at your altar:

1. Light a candle and hold a piece of petrified wood or amber.
2. Close your eyes and visualize roots growing from your feet into the Earth.
3. Say:
   "Earth of old, steady and wise,
   Ground my spirit, let me rise."

2. Manifestation Ritual

Use your altar to set and amplify intentions:

1. Write your intention on a piece of paper and place it under a fossil.
2. Light a green or gold candle to symbolize growth and success.
3. Meditate on your intention, visualizing it coming to fruition with the power of prehistoric energy.

3. Cleansing and Renewal

Cleanse your altar regularly to maintain its energy:

1. Smudge the altar with sage, cedar, or palo santo.
2. Clean and rearrange items to refresh their energy.
3. Sprinkle salt or place crystals like selenite on the altar to absorb negativity.

Daily Maintenance of Your Prehistoric Altar

1. **Keep It Clean:** Dust and organize the altar regularly to maintain its sacredness.
2. **Revisit Intentions:** Periodically update or replace objects to reflect new goals or cycles.
3. **Offerings:** Leave small offerings, such as water, seeds, or flowers, to honor the Earth and its ancient energies.

Magickal Benefits of a Prehistoric Altar

- **Enhanced Focus:** Provides a dedicated space for magickal work, increasing your focus and intention.
- **Connection to Ancient Energy:** Strengthens your bond with prehistoric wisdom and Earth's history.
- **Amplified Rituals:** Fossils and sacred objects amplify the energy of your spells and meditations.
- **Grounding and Stability:** Anchors your practice in the steady energy of the Earth.

Closing Thoughts on Prehistoric Altars

A prehistoric altar is more than a physical space—it is a bridge to the ancient world, a tool for channeling Earth's primal energy, and a reflection of your magickal journey. By dedicating time and intention to its creation and care, you can deepen your connection to prehistoric magick and enhance your spiritual practice.

Let this altar become your sanctuary as you continue to explore **The Dino Grimoire**, drawing strength, wisdom, and inspiration from the ancient forces that shaped our world.

Chapter 25: Ancient Ocean Energies and Marine Dinosaurs

The prehistoric oceans were teeming with life, from colossal marine reptiles like Plesiosaurs and Mosasaurs to the ammonites and trilobites that flourished beneath the waves. These ancient waters, vast and mysterious, were both a cradle of life and a realm of primal power. The magick of the pre-historic oceans offers a deep connection to the elements of water, the mysteries of transformation, and the cycles of life and death. By working with the energies of ancient seas and their marine inhabitants, practitioners can harness the power of fluidity, adaptability, and profound wisdom.

This chapter explores the energies of prehistoric oceans and provides rituals, meditations, and practices to connect with marine dinosaurs and ancient aquatic life.

The Magick of Prehistoric Oceans

The prehistoric oceans were dynamic, life-giving environments that shaped the evolution of countless species. Their energy reflects powerful themes in magick:

1. **Transformation:** The constant motion of waves and currents symbolizes change and adaptability.
2. **Depth and Mystery:** The vast, unexplored depths represent the subconscious and hidden truths.
3. **Life and Renewal:** Oceans are the origin of life, embodying creation, fertility, and growth.
4. **Cleansing and Healing:** The waters of ancient seas carry the power to cleanse negativity and heal emotional wounds.

Marine Dinosaurs and Their Symbolism

Marine reptiles like Plesiosaurs and Mosasaurs were apex predators of the prehistoric seas, each carrying unique energies that can enhance your magickal practice:

1. Plesiosaur

- **Symbolism:** Grace, intuition, and connection to the unknown.
- **Energy:** The Plesiosaur's long neck and graceful movements symbolize fluidity and heightened intuition. Its connection to deep waters makes it an ideal guide for exploring the subconscious.
- **Magickal Focus:** Use Plesiosaur energy in dreamwork, intuition, and emotional healing.

2. Mosasaur

- **Symbolism:** Power, adaptability, and transformation.
- **Energy:** As a dominant predator, the Mosasaur embodies strength and the ability to adapt to shifting environments. Its swift and decisive nature is ideal for achieving goals and overcoming obstacles.
- **Magickal Focus:** Work with Mosasaur energy for empowerment, success, and courage.

3. Ammonites

- **Symbolism:** Cycles, protection, and evolution.
- **Energy:** These coiled shells are symbols of life's cycles and the protective embrace of nature. Ammonites also represent transformation and balance.
- **Magickal Focus:** Use ammonite energy in rituals for protection, grounding, and alignment with natural rhythms.

4. Trilobites

- **Symbolism:** Resilience, adaptability, and ancient wisdom.
- **Energy:** These early arthropods survived for millions of years, embodying endurance and the wisdom of persistence.
- **Magickal Focus:** Work with trilobite energy to strengthen resilience and adapt to change.

Working with Ancient Ocean Energies
1. Elemental Water Connection
The prehistoric ocean is a manifestation of the element of water, representing emotions, intuition, and flow. Connect to this energy by spending time near natural bodies of water, such as oceans, lakes, or rivers.
Practice:

1. Stand by the water and close your eyes.
2. Visualize yourself in a prehistoric ocean, surrounded by ancient creatures like Plesiosaurs and ammonites.
3. Feel the energy of the water washing over you, cleansing and renewing your spirit.

2. Fossils and Marine Symbols
Incorporate fossils of marine creatures into your practice to channel the energy of the prehistoric seas.
Suggestions:

- Use ammonite fossils for cycles and transformation.
- Work with fossilized coral for emotional healing and connection.
- Include trilobite fossils for grounding and resilience.

Rituals for Harnessing Ancient Ocean Energies
1. Emotional Healing Ritual: Plesiosaur's Grace
This ritual uses the gentle and intuitive energy of the Plesiosaur to heal emotional wounds and restore balance.
Materials Needed:

- A fossilized ammonite or shell.
- A blue or teal candle.
- A bowl of salt water.

Steps:

1. Light the blue candle and place the fossil beside the bowl of salt water.
2. Hold the fossil and close your eyes, visualizing a Plesiosaur gliding gracefully through the water.
3. Chant:
   "Guardian of oceans, gentle and wise,
   Heal my heart, soothe my cries.
   Through ancient waters, let pain be freed,
   With your grace, fulfill my need."
4. Dip your hands into the salt water, allowing it to absorb your emotional burdens.

2. Manifestation Ritual: Mosasaur's Power
Invoke the strength and adaptability of the Mosasaur to achieve your goals and overcome obstacles.
Materials Needed:

- A fossilized tooth or claw (or a sharp crystal like obsidian).
- A red or gold candle.
- A piece of paper and pen.

Steps:

1. Write your goal or intention on the paper.
2. Light the candle and hold the fossil or crystal in your hand.
3. Visualize the Mosasaur swimming powerfully through the water, clearing obstacles in its path.
4. Chant:
   "Mosasaur, swift and strong,
   Grant me power to right the wrong.

Through ancient seas, I take my place,
With your might, I'll win the race."

5. Burn the paper in the candle flame, releasing your intention into the universe.

3. Protection Ritual: Ammonite Shield

Create a protective energy shield using the coiled power of ammonites.

Materials Needed:

- An ammonite fossil.
- A black candle.
- A circle of salt or stones.

Steps:

1. Place the ammonite fossil in the center of the salt circle.
2. Light the black candle and visualize a glowing spiral of energy forming around you, inspired by the ammonite's shape.
3. Chant:
   "Ammonite ancient, shield of old,
   Protect my space, strong and bold.
   Encircle me with your timeless grace,
   Guard my heart, my sacred space."
4. Keep the ammonite on your altar or carry it with you for ongoing protection.

Meditations with Marine Dinosaurs
Plesiosaur Meditation: Exploring the Depths

Use this meditation to access your subconscious and uncover hidden truths.

1. Sit in a quiet space with a fossil or shell.
2. Close your eyes and visualize yourself diving into a prehistoric ocean.
3. Imagine a Plesiosaur guiding you through underwater caves and currents, revealing symbols or messages.
4. When ready, return to the surface and journal your experience.

Mosasaur Meditation: Empowerment and Action

Channel the Mosasaur's energy to boost confidence and courage.

1. Hold a fossilized tooth or sharp crystal in your hand.
2. Visualize a Mosasaur moving powerfully through the ocean, embodying strength and determination.
3. Breathe deeply, imagining its energy flowing into you, filling you with boldness and clarity.

Daily Practices for Ancient Ocean Magick

1. **Fossil Carrying:** Keep a small ammonite or trilobite fossil with you to maintain a connection to ancient ocean energies.
2. **Moonlit Water Rituals:** Work with ocean energy during the Full Moon by meditating near water or charging fossils in moonlight.
3. **Salt Water Cleansing:** Use salt water to cleanse your tools and yourself, invoking the purifying energy of prehistoric seas.

Magickal Benefits of Ancient Ocean Energies

- **Emotional Balance:** Prehistoric waters bring calm and healing to turbulent emotions.
- **Adaptability:** Marine creatures like Mosasaurs inspire resilience and quick thinking.
- **Connection to Subconscious:** The depth of ancient oceans mirrors the depth of the psyche, providing access to hidden wisdom.
- **Empowerment:** The strength of marine dinosaurs boosts confidence and determination.

Honoring Ancient Ocean Energies in Your Practice

By working with fossils, symbols, and rituals inspired by prehistoric oceans, you can deepen your connection to the primal forces of water and marine life. This practice not only enhances your magickal abilities but also fosters a profound appreciation for Earth's ancient history and the life it nurtured.

Let the timeless energy of prehistoric seas guide your magick as you explore **The Dino Grimoire**, unlocking the mysteries of the ancient oceans and their majestic inhabitants.

Chapter 26: Dino Shapeshifting Rituals

Shapeshifting is one of the most ancient and powerful practices in magick, allowing the practitioner to embody the essence of another being. Dino shapeshifting rituals focus on channeling the spirit and energy of prehistoric creatures, temporarily transforming your aura and mindset to align with their unique strengths, qualities, and abilities. Whether you seek the strength of a Tyrannosaurus Rex, the cunning of a Velociraptor, or the grace of a Plesiosaur, these rituals enable you to access the primal power of dinosaurs for protection, guidance, and personal empowerment.

This chapter provides detailed guidance on preparing for shapeshifting, performing dino shapeshifting rituals, and integrating this energy into your magickal and daily life.

The Magick of Dino Shapeshifting

Shapeshifting does not involve physical transformation but rather a profound energetic and spiritual alignment with a chosen dinosaur's essence. This practice can enhance your magickal abilities and deepen your connection to prehistoric energies.

Benefits of Dino Shapeshifting

1. **Strength and Courage:** Channel the physical power of dinosaurs to overcome challenges.
2. **Adaptability:** Learn to navigate complex situations with the resourcefulness of ancient creatures.
3. **Connection to Nature:** Deepen your bond with Earth's primal energies.
4. **Spiritual Guidance:** Gain insights and wisdom from the spirit of your chosen dinosaur.

Preparing for Shapeshifting Rituals

To successfully embody the spirit of a dinosaur, preparation is essential:

1. Choose Your Dinosaur

Each dinosaur carries unique energies and attributes. Select one that aligns with your intention:

- **Tyrannosaurus Rex:** For strength, dominance, and protection.
- **Triceratops:** For grounding, stability, and resilience.
- **Velociraptor:** For agility, strategy, and quick thinking.
- **Plesiosaur:** For intuition, grace, and emotional healing.
- **Brachiosaurus:** For growth, patience, and endurance.

2. Gather Ritual Tools

- **A Fossil or Symbolic Item:** Representing your chosen dinosaur (e.g., a dinosaur tooth, claw fossil, or figurine).
- **Candles:** Use colors that correspond to your intention (e.g., red for strength, blue for intuition).
- **Incense or Herbs:** Select scents that align with your ritual (e.g., cedar for grounding, sage for cleansing).

- **Drumming or Music:** Rhythmic sounds help induce a trance-like state.

3. Create a Sacred Space

- Cleanse the space with smoke, salt, or sound to ensure it is free of negative energy.
- Arrange your altar with fossils, candles, and symbols of your chosen dinosaur.

4. Ground and Center Yourself

Before beginning the ritual, perform a grounding exercise to connect to the Earth's energy and prepare your body and mind for transformation.

Dino Shapeshifting Rituals

1. Strength and Protection: Tyrannosaurus Rex Transformation

Purpose: Embody the strength and fearlessness of the T-Rex for protection and empowerment.

Materials Needed:

- A red candle.
- A dinosaur tooth or claw fossil.
- Drumming or rhythmic music.

Steps:

1. Light the red candle and place the fossil in front of you.
2. Begin drumming or playing rhythmic music to establish a steady beat.
3. Close your eyes and visualize a Tyrannosaurus Rex standing tall and powerful before you. Feel its immense strength and protective energy.
4. Chant:
   "Tyrant King, fierce and true,
   Lend me strength to see it through.
   Fearless guardian, bold and great,
   Protect my path, control my fate."
5. As you chant, imagine the T-Rex's spirit merging with your own. Feel its energy coursing through your body, empowering you.
6. When ready, extinguish the candle and carry the fossil with you as a talisman of protection.

2. Agility and Strategy: Velociraptor Shapeshifting

Purpose: Harness the cunning and agility of the Velociraptor for quick thinking and strategic action.

Materials Needed:

- A green or yellow candle.
- A small, sharp fossil or crystal (e.g., obsidian or quartz).
- A feather or symbolic representation of speed.

Steps:

1. Light the candle and hold the fossil or crystal in your hand.
2. Visualize a Velociraptor moving swiftly and gracefully through its environment. Feel its sharp intelligence and strategic focus.

3. Chant:
"Velociraptor, agile and wise,
Quick of thought, sharp of eyes.
Guide my steps, my mind and speed,
With your wit, fulfill my need."

4. Begin to move, mimicking the swift, precise movements of the Velociraptor. Let its energy flow through you.
5. End the ritual by placing the feather on your altar as a symbol of the transformation.

3. Emotional Healing and Intuition: Plesiosaur Shapeshifting

Purpose: Connect with the intuitive and healing energy of the Plesiosaur to restore emotional balance.

Materials Needed:

- A blue candle.
- A bowl of water.
- A shell fossil or smooth stone.

Steps:

1. Light the blue candle and place the bowl of water in front of you.
2. Hold the shell fossil or stone and close your eyes. Visualize a Plesiosaur gliding through calm waters, its presence serene and nurturing.
3. Chant:
"Plesiosaur, graceful and deep,
Guide my heart, my pain to keep.
Heal my soul, restore my peace,
Intuition's flow, let it increase."

4. Dip your hands into the water, imagining the Plesiosaur's energy washing over you, cleansing emotional wounds.
5. End the ritual by placing the fossil or stone on your altar as a reminder of healing.

4. Growth and Patience: Brachiosaurus Transformation

Purpose: Embody the steady and enduring energy of the Brachiosaurus for long-term goals and growth.

Materials Needed:

- A green candle.
- A piece of petrified wood or large stone.
- A small potted plant or tree branch.

Steps:

1. Light the green candle and place the petrified wood or stone beside the plant.
2. Visualize a Brachiosaurus moving slowly and steadily through a prehistoric forest, its presence calm and patient.
3. Chant:
   "Brachiosaurus, steady and tall,
   Teach me patience, through it all.
   Growth and wisdom, strong and slow,
   Like the forest, help me grow."
4. Focus on the plant as a symbol of your own growth, imagining roots extending deep into the Earth.
5. End the ritual by placing the plant on your altar or caring for it as a living representation of your transformation.

Daily Practices to Strengthen Shapeshifting

1. **Morning Invocation:** Begin each day by invoking the energy of your chosen dinosaur with a short chant or meditation.
2. **Movement Practices:** Mimic the movements of your chosen dinosaur to internalize its energy (e.g., slow, steady steps for a Brachiosaurus, swift and sharp movements for a Velociraptor).
3. **Talisman Carrying:** Keep a fossil or symbolic item with you to maintain the connection to your dinosaur's spirit.

After the Ritual: Grounding and Reflection

After a shapeshifting ritual, it's important to ground yourself and reflect on the experience:

1. **Grounding:** Place your hands on the Earth or hold a grounding stone like hematite. Breathe deeply to return fully to your body.
2. **Reflection:** Journal your experience, noting any insights, emotions, or changes in energy.

Magickal Benefits of Dino Shapeshifting

- **Empowerment:** Gain confidence and strength through your connection to powerful prehistoric energies.
- **Adaptability:** Enhance your ability to navigate challenges with resilience and grace.
- **Deepened Intuition:** Access hidden knowledge and spiritual guidance from the dinosaur spirit.
- **Spiritual Growth:** Strengthen your bond with Earth's ancient forces, enriching your magickal practice.

Conclusion: Transforming Through Prehistoric Power

Dino shapeshifting rituals offer a unique and powerful way to channel the ancient energies of Earth's most awe-inspiring creatures. By temporarily embodying the spirit of a dinosaur, you can access its strengths, qualities, and wisdom, empowering your magickal journey and personal growth.

Let these transformative rituals guide you as you delve deeper into **The Dino Grimoire**, awakening the primal power within and unlocking the mysteries of prehistoric magick.

Chapter 27: Volcanoes and Magma Spells

Volcanoes, the fiery forges of the Earth, have shaped the planet's landscapes for billions of years. In the prehistoric world, volcanic eruptions were both destructive and life-giving, creating fertile soils and influencing the evolution of life. Volcanoes are primal sources of raw power, representing transformation, creation, destruction, and renewal. By working with volcanic energy, you can harness these forces for powerful magickal purposes, including manifestation, purification, and empowerment.

This chapter explores the magickal significance of volcanoes and magma, provides guidance on channeling their energy, and offers rituals and spells to incorporate this ancient force into your magickal practice.

The Magickal Significance of Volcanoes

Volcanoes are dynamic symbols of transformation and raw elemental power. Their magickal significance includes:

1. **Creation and Destruction:** Volcanoes destroy as they erupt but also create new land and fertile soil, embodying the cycles of death and rebirth.
2. **Fire and Earth Elements:** As a merging of fire and earth energies, volcanoes represent both passion and stability, making them ideal for transformative magick.
3. **Primal Power:** Their raw, untamed energy connects to the primal forces of the Earth, allowing for powerful manifestations and breakthroughs.
4. **Renewal:** The cooling and hardening of lava symbolize the solidification of intentions and the grounding of energy.

Volcanic Energy in Prehistoric Times

In the prehistoric world, volcanic eruptions shaped ecosystems, influenced weather patterns, and contributed to mass extinctions and evolutionary bursts. This connection to cycles of change and resilience makes volcanic energy a potent force for magickal workings:

- **Prehistoric Volcanoes:** Massive volcanic eruptions created vast lava plains and reshaped continents, influencing the habitats of dinosaurs and early life.
- **Fossilized Lava:** Rocks formed from ancient lava flows carry the energy of these primordial events, making them powerful tools in magick.

Magickal Correspondences of Volcanoes

Aspect	Symbolism	Uses in Magick
Lava (Magma)	Raw power, transformation	Manifestation, destruction of obstacles
Ash	Renewal, fertility	Grounding, creating fertile energy
Volcanic Stones	Stability, grounding	Anchoring intentions, protection
Eruptions	Release, breakthroughs	Overcoming challenges, releasing energy

Volcanic Magick Tools

Incorporate volcanic materials into your practice to harness their energy:

1. **Obsidian:** Formed from rapidly cooled lava, obsidian is a powerful tool for protection, transformation, and cutting away negativity.
2. **Basalt:** A volcanic rock representing grounding and stability.
3. **Pumice:** A lightweight volcanic stone used for purification and releasing burdens.
4. **Volcanic Ash:** Represents renewal and fertility, ideal for grounding spells.

Preparing for Volcano and Magma Spells

Before working with volcanic energy, take the following steps:

1. **Set Your Intention:** Define the purpose of your spell, such as transformation, release, or empowerment.
2. **Cleanse Your Space:** Use smoke, sound, or salt to prepare your ritual area.
3. **Choose Your Tools:** Gather volcanic stones, candles, and other ritual items that align with your intention.
4. **Create a Sacred Space:** Arrange your tools on an altar or in a circle, incorporating fiery elements like red candles or warm-colored fabrics.

Volcano and Magma Spells
1. Magma Manifestation Spell
Purpose: Channel the raw, creative energy of magma to manifest your desires.
Materials Needed:

- A piece of basalt or obsidian.
- A red or orange candle.
- A piece of paper and pen.

Steps:

1. Light the candle and hold the basalt or obsidian in your hand.
2. Write your intention or goal on the paper, focusing on the energy of creation and transformation.
3. Visualize magma flowing beneath the Earth, carrying the energy of your intention. Imagine it rising and solidifying into reality.
4. Chant:
   "From the Earth's fiery core, I call,
   Manifest my will, let it enthrall.
   Lava's flow, intention bright,
   Solidify now, through Earth's might."
5. Burn the paper in the candle flame (safely) and bury the ashes in the ground to ground your intention.

2. Eruption Release Ritual

Purpose: Release negativity, emotional blockages, or obstacles.
Materials Needed:

- A small piece of pumice.
- A black candle.
- A bowl of water.

Steps:

1. Light the black candle and hold the pumice, focusing on what you wish to release.
2. Visualize a volcanic eruption, with lava breaking through and clearing away all negativity.
3. Chant:
   "Volcano's fire, fierce and free,
   Burn away what burdens me.
   Through ash and flame, I let it go,
   Renewal comes, through magma's flow."
4. Drop the pumice into the bowl of water, symbolizing the cooling and solidification of your release.
5. Dispose of the water and pumice, thanking the volcanic energy for its aid.

3. Lava Shield Spell

Purpose: Create a protective barrier using the energy of lava and volcanic stones.
Materials Needed:

- A piece of obsidian or basalt.
- A circle of red or black candles.
- Volcanic ash (optional).

Steps:

1. Arrange the candles in a circle around you and light them.
2. Hold the obsidian or basalt in your hand and visualize a shield of glowing lava forming around you, impenetrable and protective.
3. Chant:
   "From Earth's core, a shield I weave,
   Protection strong, I now receive.
   Lava's flow, fierce and bright,
   Guard my spirit, day and night."
4. Sprinkle volcanic ash around the circle (optional) to seal the protective energy.

5. Extinguish the candles and carry the obsidian or basalt as a protective talisman.

4. Fertility and Renewal Spell
Purpose: Harness volcanic ash for growth, renewal, and fertility.
Materials Needed:

- A small jar of volcanic ash.
- A green candle.
- A small plant or seedling.

Steps:

1. Light the green candle and place the volcanic ash beside the plant or seedling.
2. Sprinkle the ash into the soil, visualizing it infusing the Earth with fertile energy.
3. Chant:
   "Volcanic ash, fertile and old,
   Bring forth life, let it unfold.
   Growth and renewal, strong and pure,
   Through ancient power, life will endure."
4. Care for the plant as a living symbol of your spell.

Volcano Meditation
Meditate to connect with the energy of volcanoes and magma:

1. Sit comfortably with a piece of obsidian or basalt in your hand.
2. Close your eyes and visualize yourself standing at the base of an ancient volcano, feeling its heat and power.
3. Imagine magma flowing beneath the surface, carrying raw energy.
4. Focus on the energy rising within you, fueling your intention and filling you with strength.

Daily Practices to Honor Volcanic Energy

1. **Carry Volcanic Stones:** Keep obsidian, basalt, or pumice with you as talismans of strength and transformation.
2. **Use Volcanic Ash:** Incorporate ash into rituals or sprinkle it around sacred spaces for renewal.
3. **Fire Element Focus:** Light red or orange candles to honor the fiery energy of volcanoes.
4. **Grounding Walks:** Spend time in volcanic regions or areas with igneous rocks to connect with Earth's primal energy.

Magickal Benefits of Volcanic Energy

- **Empowerment:** Tap into the raw, untamed energy of the Earth for strength and confidence.
- **Transformation:** Use the cycles of eruption and renewal to create profound change in your life.
- **Protection:** Create fiery shields of protection against negativity and harm.
- **Manifestation:** Channel the creative force of magma to solidify your goals and intentions.

Closing Thoughts on Volcano and Magma Spells

Volcanoes are primal symbols of transformation, embodying the raw power of the Earth's core. By channeling volcanic energy, you can access an unparalleled source of magickal strength and creativity. Whether you seek to manifest your desires, release negativity, or protect yourself, volcanic magick offers a dynamic and powerful path.

Let the fiery energy of prehistoric volcanoes inspire your magick as you explore **The Dino Grimoire**, unlocking the transformative power of Earth's most ancient forces.

Chapter 28: Meteoric Energy and Cosmic Magick

Meteoric impacts have shaped the Earth's history, from carving vast craters to contributing to mass extinctions, such as the one that ended the age of the dinosaurs. These celestial events are reminders of the interconnectedness between Earth and the cosmos. In magick, meteoric energy represents transformation, cosmic insight, and immense power. The ancient forces unleashed by meteors can be harnessed to enhance spellwork, connect with universal energies, and align with celestial rhythms.

This chapter delves into the significance of meteoric energy, its role in shaping the prehistoric world, and how to work with it for powerful cosmic magick.

The Magickal Significance of Meteoric Energy

Meteorites are fragments of celestial bodies that have journeyed through space and crashed onto Earth. Their magickal significance lies in their dual nature as both cosmic and terrestrial:

1. **Cosmic Connection:** Meteorites are born in the vastness of space, carrying the energy of stars, planets, and the universe itself.
2. **Transformation:** The impact of a meteorite symbolizes profound change, destruction, and renewal.
3. **Celestial Insight:** Meteoric energy offers access to universal wisdom and the mysteries of the cosmos.
4. **Rare and Unique Power:** Each meteorite carries a distinct energy, shaped by its origin and journey.

Meteoric Impacts in Prehistoric Times

Meteoric impacts played a significant role in shaping the prehistoric world:

1. **Mass Extinction Events:** The Chicxulub meteor impact, approximately 66 million years ago, is widely believed to have caused the extinction of the dinosaurs, paving the way for the rise of mammals.
2. **Geological Transformation:** Meteor impacts created craters, shifted ecosystems, and influenced the planet's evolution.

3. **Elemental Infusion:** Meteorites introduced rare elements and minerals to Earth, enriching its composition and influencing its energy.

These events highlight the transformative and powerful nature of meteoric energy, making it a potent force in magickal practice.

Magickal Correspondences of Meteoric Energy

Aspect	Symbolism	Uses in Magick
Meteorites	Cosmic connection, insight	Universal wisdom, astral travel
Impact Craters	Transformation, renewal	Breaking cycles, starting anew
Falling Stars (Meteors)	Wishes, divine intervention	Manifestation, goal setting
Celestial Metals (e.g., Iron)	Strength, grounding	Protection, energy amplification

Meteorite Types and Their Magickal Properties

Different types of meteorites carry unique energies that can be used in magickal practices:

1. **Iron Meteorites**
   - **Energy:** Strength, grounding, and focus.
   - **Uses:** Protection, stability, and anchoring celestial energy.
2. **Stony Meteorites**
   - **Energy:** Connection to Earth and cosmos, transformation.
   - **Uses:** Manifestation, alignment with cosmic rhythms, and personal growth.
3. **Pallasites (Stony-Iron Meteorites)**
   - **Energy:** Rare and powerful balance of cosmic and terrestrial forces.
   - **Uses:** Duality work, balance, and integration of higher energies.
4. **Tektites**
   - **Energy:** Amplification, astral travel, and insight.
   - **Uses:** Enhancing intuition, connecting with higher realms, and spiritual evolution.

Preparing for Cosmic Magick

To work effectively with meteoric energy, preparation is key:

1. Gather Materials

- **Meteorites or Tektites:** These can be authentic fragments or symbolic representations.
- **Candles:** Use colors like silver (cosmic energy), black (transformation), or blue (insight).
- **Celestial Charts:** To align your work with astrological or lunar phases.
- **Incense or Oils:** Scents like frankincense or myrrh evoke celestial energy.

2. Cleanse and Charge Meteorites

- Cleanse the meteorite with smoke, salt, or moonlight to remove residual energy.
- Charge it with your intention by holding it and visualizing its cosmic energy radiating outward.

3. Create a Sacred Space

- Arrange your tools in a circle, incorporating celestial symbols such as stars, constellations, or planetary representations.

Meteoric Energy Rituals
1. Cosmic Manifestation Spell
Purpose: Harness the energy of meteoric impacts to manifest your goals with cosmic power.
Materials Needed:

- A stony meteorite or tektite.
- A silver candle.
- A piece of paper and pen.

Steps:

1. Light the silver candle and hold the meteorite in your hand.
2. Write your goal on the paper, focusing on its manifestation with cosmic support.
3. Visualize the meteorite's energy connecting with the universe, drawing your goal closer to reality.
4. Chant:
   "From the stars to the Earth below,
   Cosmic forces, let my will flow.
   Through meteoric fire, my path is clear,
   Manifest my goal, bring it near."
5. Burn the paper in the candle flame and scatter the ashes outside, releasing your intention to the universe.

2. Transformation and Renewal Ritual
Purpose: Use meteoric energy to release old patterns and embrace transformation.
Materials Needed:

- An iron meteorite or symbolic stone.
- A black candle.
- A bowl of water.

Steps:

1. Light the black candle and place the meteorite in the bowl of water.
2. Visualize the meteorite's impact energy breaking through obstacles in your life.
3. Chant:
   "Cosmic stone, forged in fire,
   Break the chains, lift me higher.
   From destruction, renewal springs,
   Transform my life, on cosmic wings."

4. Dip your hands into the water, imagining the release of negativity and the flow of transformative energy.

3. Astral Travel and Insight Spell

Purpose: Connect with cosmic realms for guidance and spiritual growth.
Materials Needed:

- A tektite or celestial stone.
- A blue or purple candle.
- Incense (e.g., frankincense).

Steps:

1. Light the candle and incense, holding the tektite in your hand.
2. Close your eyes and visualize yourself traveling through space, guided by the meteorite's energy.
3. Chant:
    "Celestial guide, from starry sea,
    Show the paths of destiny.
    Through astral realms, my spirit flies,
    Cosmic truth, open my eyes."
4. Spend time meditating, allowing images, symbols, or messages to come through.

4. Protection Spell: Meteoric Shield

Purpose: Create a protective barrier using the strength of meteoric energy.
Materials Needed:

- An iron meteorite or basalt.
- A circle of black candles.
- A pinch of salt or volcanic ash.

Steps:

1. Arrange the candles in a circle around you and light them.
2. Hold the meteorite and visualize a glowing shield forming around you, infused with cosmic energy.
3. Sprinkle the salt or ash around the circle, sealing the protective barrier.
4. Chant:
    "From star to Earth, energy strong,
    Protect my spirit, all day long.

Cosmic shield, bright and pure,
Guard my path, keep me secure."

5. Keep the meteorite on your altar or carry it as a talisman.

Daily Practices with Meteoric Energy

1. **Carry Meteoric Stones:** Keep a small meteorite or tektite with you to maintain a connection to cosmic energy.
2. **Night Sky Meditation:** Spend time under the stars, focusing on your bond with the universe.
3. **Align with Celestial Events:** Perform rituals during meteor showers, eclipses, or significant astrological alignments for amplified power.

Magickal Benefits of Meteoric Energy

- **Universal Wisdom:** Gain insights and guidance from the cosmos.
- **Transformation:** Harness meteoric impacts for personal and spiritual evolution.
- **Protection:** Create strong, celestial shields against negativity.
- **Manifestation:** Amplify your intentions with the power of cosmic energy.

The Legacy of Cosmic Magick

Meteorites are reminders of the vastness of the universe and its influence on Earth's history. By working with meteoric energy, you can align your magickal practice with the cosmos, accessing the transformative and powerful forces that shaped the prehistoric world.

Let meteoric energy guide your journey as you explore **The Dino Grimoire**, unlocking the mysteries of the stars and their profound connection to our planet.

Chapter 29: Dinosaur-Inspired Sigils

Sigils are powerful magickal symbols created to manifest specific intentions. Combining the timeless art of sigil creation with the primal energies of dinosaurs allows practitioners to craft unique and potent symbols that carry the strength, resilience, and wisdom of prehistoric life. Dinosaur-inspired sigils utilize shapes, symbols, and features associated with specific dinosaurs to amplify intentions and align with their distinctive energies.

This chapter explores the principles of sigil creation, how to design dinosaur-inspired sigils, and methods to activate and use them in your magickal practice.

The Magick of Sigils and Dinosaurs

Sigils are personalized symbols that encode an intention or desire into a visual representation. By merging sigil magick with dinosaur symbolism, you tap into:

1. **Primal Energy:** Dinosaurs symbolize raw power, endurance, and adaptability, enhancing the potency of your sigils.
2. **Focused Intentions:** Sigils channel the unique qualities of dinosaurs, such as strength (Tyrannosaurus Rex), agility (Velociraptor), or protection (Triceratops).
3. **Ancient Connection:** Dinosaur shapes and features create a link to Earth's prehistoric past, grounding your magick in primal energy.

Steps to Create Dinosaur-Inspired Sigils

1. Define Your Intention

Begin by clearly stating your goal or desire. This could be a single word (e.g., "Protection") or a full sentence (e.g., "I am protected and resilient in all situations").

Examples of Intentions:

- Strength and courage (Tyrannosaurus Rex)
- Focus and agility (Velociraptor)
- Grounding and stability (Brachiosaurus)
- Protection and shielding (Triceratops)

2. Choose a Dinosaur for Symbolic Energy

Select a dinosaur that aligns with your intention. Understanding their symbolism will help you incorporate meaningful elements into your sigil:

- **Tyrannosaurus Rex:** Strength, dominance, and leadership.
- **Triceratops:** Protection, defense, and stability.
- **Velociraptor:** Agility, strategy, and quick thinking.
- **Stegosaurus:** Shielding, resilience, and patience.

- **Pterodactyl:** Freedom, perspective, and spiritual elevation.
- **Brachiosaurus:** Growth, long-term planning, and endurance.

3. Break Down Your Intention

Reduce your intention into key letters or shapes to form the foundation of your sigil.

Example:

Intention: "I am resilient and protected."

- Remove vowels and repeating letters: **RSLNT PRCTD**

4. Incorporate Dinosaur Shapes

Use features of your chosen dinosaur to shape your sigil. Focus on iconic elements such as:

- **Tyrannosaurus Rex:** Sharp teeth, powerful legs, or a roaring jaw.
- **Triceratops:** Horns, frill, or sturdy legs.
- **Velociraptor:** Clawed feet, sleek body, or a curved tail.
- **Pterodactyl:** Wings, beak, or aerial poses.
- **Brachiosaurus:** Long neck, broad body, or steady feet.

5. Combine Elements into a Unified Symbol

Blend the letters and shapes into a cohesive design. Experiment with lines, curves, and geometric patterns to create a visually appealing sigil.

Example:

For protection and resilience using Triceratops energy:

- Begin with a circular shape for shielding.
- Incorporate horn-like spikes or triangles for defense.
- Integrate parts of the letters **R**, **S**, and **T** into the design for added symbolism.

Activating Your Dinosaur-Inspired Sigil
Once your sigil is complete, activate it to infuse it with magickal energy.
1. Charging with Energy

- **Meditation:** Hold the sigil in your hands and visualize energy flowing into it, imbuing it with your intention.
- **Elements:** Charge the sigil using natural elements, such as burying it in soil, holding it in sunlight, or passing it through smoke or flame.

2. Visualization Ritual

1. Place the sigil on your altar or a sacred space.
2. Light a candle that corresponds to your intention (e.g., red for strength, green for growth).
3. Focus on the sigil, visualizing your intention as a glowing light emanating from it.
4. Chant:
   "Through ancient force, my will is clear,
   Dinosaur strength, draw it near.
   Sigil crafted, power flow,
   Let my intention brightly glow."

3. Burning for Manifestation
For intentions you wish to send into the universe:

1. Draw the sigil on paper.
2. Burn it in a fire-safe dish, visualizing the energy being released into the cosmos.

Using Dinosaur-Inspired Sigils

Once activated, your sigil can be used in various ways to enhance your magickal practice:

1. Carry It as a Talisman

Draw the sigil on a small piece of paper, wood, or stone and keep it with you for ongoing protection, strength, or focus.

2. Add to Spellwork

Incorporate your sigil into rituals by carving it onto candles, drawing it on petition papers, or inscribing it into wax or clay.

3. Meditate with the Sigil

Focus on the sigil during meditation to connect with the energy of the dinosaur it represents.

4. Place It on Your Altar

Display the sigil on your altar as a focal point for your magickal intentions.

5. Use It in Visualization

Visualize the sigil glowing and activating whenever you need its energy.

Examples of Dinosaur-Inspired Sigils

1. Tyrannosaurus Rex (Strength and Courage)

- Sharp, angular lines resembling teeth and claws.
- A bold, triangular base for stability.

2. Triceratops (Protection)

- Circular shield with three outward-facing spikes.
- Wavy lines representing resilience.

3. Velociraptor (Focus and Agility)

- Sleek, curved lines mimicking a raptor's tail and claws.
- Spiraling elements to represent quick movement.

4. Pterodactyl (Freedom and Perspective)

- Wing-like shapes extending upward.
- A central triangle representing elevated vision.

Sigil Maintenance and Renewal

1. **Recharging:** Periodically recharge your sigil using the elements or by revisiting the activation ritual.
2. **Updating Intentions:** If your intention evolves, modify the sigil or create a new one to align with your updated goals.
3. **Cleansing:** Cleanse the sigil to remove residual energies before reactivation.

Magickal Benefits of Dinosaur-Inspired Sigils

- **Strengthened Intentions:** Sigils focus and amplify your desires, making them more effective.
- **Personalized Energy:** Incorporating dinosaur symbolism creates a unique connection to prehistoric power.
- **Versatility:** Sigils can be used in spellwork, meditation, or as talismans.
- **Timeless Power:** Dinosaur-inspired sigils draw on ancient energy, adding depth and resonance to your magick.

Final Thoughts on Dinosaur-Inspired Sigils

Dinosaur-inspired sigils merge the ancient power of prehistoric creatures with the modern practice of sigil magick. By integrating their unique energies and symbolism into your sigils, you create potent tools for transformation, protection, and manifestation. These sigils not only amplify your magickal intentions but also honor the primal forces that shaped the Earth.

Let your sigils guide and empower you as you explore **The Dino Grimoire**, unlocking the enduring strength and wisdom of the prehistoric world.

Chapter 30: Prehistoric Shadow Work

The prehistoric world was a realm of both awe-inspiring wonders and formidable challenges. Just as ancient creatures navigated a landscape of survival and transformation, so too do we carry within us shadows—those hidden, often suppressed aspects of ourselves that influence our thoughts, emotions, and behaviors. Prehistoric shadow work involves delving into these darker facets, using the primal energies of prehistoric magick to illuminate, understand, and integrate them for personal growth and self-discovery.

This chapter explores the concept of shadow work through the lens of prehistoric magick, offering techniques, rituals, and practices to confront and embrace your inner shadows, transforming them into sources of strength and wisdom.

Understanding Shadow Work

What Is Shadow Work?

Shadow work is a psychological and spiritual practice that involves exploring the unconscious parts of the self—traits, desires, and emotions that we have repressed or denied. Coined by psychologist Carl Jung, the "shadow" represents the aspects of ourselves that we consider undesirable or unacceptable, often buried deep within our psyche.

The Importance of Shadow Work

- **Self-Awareness:** By acknowledging and understanding our shadows, we gain deeper insights into our motivations and behaviors.
- **Healing and Integration:** Confronting suppressed emotions can lead to healing past traumas and integrating fragmented parts of ourselves.
- **Personal Growth:** Embracing the shadow enhances personal development, leading to a more authentic and empowered life.
- **Enhanced Magickal Practice:** Understanding your shadow strengthens your magickal abilities by aligning your conscious and unconscious intentions.

The Prehistoric Shadow

In prehistoric magick, the shadow is symbolized by the darker aspects of the ancient world—predators, survival struggles, and natural cataclysms. These elements reflect the challenges and fears that early life forms faced, mirroring the inner battles we experience today.

Symbolism in Prehistoric Shadow Work

- **Predatory Dinosaurs (e.g., Carnotaurus, Allosaurus):** Represent inner aggression, fear, and primal instincts.
- **Extinction Events:** Symbolize profound change, loss, and the end of cycles.
- **Dark Caves and Depths:** Reflect the unconscious mind and hidden emotions.
- **Nighttime and Darkness:** Associated with mystery, the unknown, and introspection.

Preparing for Prehistoric Shadow Work
1. Create a Safe Space
Shadow work requires vulnerability and courage. Establish a safe, comfortable environment where you can explore your inner world without distractions.

- **Physical Space:** Choose a quiet room or area where you feel secure.
- **Protection:** Set up protective barriers using crystals (e.g., black tourmaline) or visualization techniques to create a safe energetic container.

2. Gather Tools and Symbols
Incorporate prehistoric elements to aid your journey:

- **Fossils:** Use fossils of predatory dinosaurs or dark-colored stones to symbolize the shadow.
- **Candles:** Black or dark-colored candles represent the unknown and can aid in focusing your intent.
- **Journal:** Keep a notebook to record insights, emotions, and reflections during your shadow work.

3. Set Intentions
Clarify your purpose for engaging in shadow work. Examples include:

- Healing past wounds.
- Understanding recurring patterns.
- Embracing suppressed emotions.

Techniques for Prehistoric Shadow Work
1. Meditation in the Ancient Cave
Purpose: Explore the depths of your unconscious mind by visualizing a journey into a prehistoric cave.
Materials Needed:

- A comfortable place to sit or lie down.
- A black candle (optional).
- A piece of obsidian or dark fossil (e.g., fossilized shark tooth).

Steps:

1. **Prepare the Space:**
    ◦ Light the black candle and place the obsidian or fossil before you.
    ◦ Dim the lights to create a cave-like atmosphere.
2. **Begin the Meditation:**
    ◦ Close your eyes and take deep, calming breaths.
    ◦ Visualize yourself standing at the entrance of a vast, ancient cave. The air is cool, and the darkness invites you inward.
3. **Journey Inward:**
    ◦ As you enter the cave, notice the textures, sounds, and sensations.
    ◦ Allow images, symbols, or feelings to emerge. These may represent aspects of your shadow.
4. **Encountering the Shadow:**
    ◦ You may meet a creature, such as a predatory dinosaur, or come across symbols that evoke strong emotions.
    ◦ Engage with these manifestations. Ask questions like:
        ▪ "What do you represent?"
        ▪ "What message do you have for me?"
5. **Returning:**
    ◦ When ready, thank any beings or symbols you've encountered.
    ◦ Retrace your steps and exit the cave, bringing with you any insights gained.
6. **Reflect:**
    ◦ Journal your experience immediately after the meditation.
    ◦ Note any emotions, thoughts, or revelations.

2. The Extinction Ritual

Purpose: Release old patterns, beliefs, or behaviors that no longer serve you, symbolizing an "extinction" of these aspects.

Materials Needed:

- A black or dark-colored candle.
- A piece of paper and pen.
- A fire-safe bowl.
- Ashes or soil (optional).

Steps:

1. **Set the Scene:**
    - Light the candle and place it on your altar or workspace.
    - Have the fire-safe bowl ready.
2. **Identify What to Release:**
    - Write down traits, habits, or beliefs you wish to let go of.
3. **Invocation:**
    - Hold the paper and say:
        - *"As the ancient cycles ended, so too shall these parts of me transform. I release what no longer serves my highest good."*
4. **Burning:**
    - Carefully burn the paper in the candle flame, placing it into the bowl.
    - Visualize these aspects dissolving, making way for new growth.
5. **Earth Integration (Optional):**
    - Mix the ashes with soil.
    - If possible, bury them in the Earth, symbolizing transformation and renewal.
6. **Closing:**
    - Extinguish the candle with gratitude.
    - Take a moment to breathe deeply and affirm your commitment to growth.

3. Dialogue with the Shadow Dinosaur

Purpose: Engage directly with your shadow by personifying it as a prehistoric creature.

Materials Needed:

- A quiet space.
- A journal and pen.
- Optional: A dinosaur figurine representing your shadow.

Steps:

1. **Visualization:**
   - Close your eyes and visualize a safe meeting place in nature.
   - Invite your shadow to appear as a dinosaur or prehistoric creature.
2. **Engagement:**
   - Observe the creature's appearance, behavior, and energy.
   - Begin a dialogue by asking questions:
     - "Who are you?"
     - "What do you need?"
     - "How can we work together?"
3. **Listening:**
   - Allow the creature to respond. This may come as thoughts, feelings, or images.
4. **Integration:**
   - Discuss ways to integrate the shadow's needs into your life.
5. **Thanking and Parting:**
   - Express gratitude for the encounter.
   - Visualize the creature returning to its realm.
6. **Journaling:**
   - Write down the conversation and any insights.

Symbols and Correspondences in Prehistoric Shadow Work

Symbol	Meaning	Usage
Obsidian	Protection, revealing truths	Scrying, grounding, and protection tools
Dark Fossils	Hidden knowledge, transformation	Meditation aids, altar pieces
Caves	Unconscious mind, introspection	Visualization spaces in meditation
Predatory Dinosaurs	Inner fears, aggression, instincts	Personifying shadows, confronting fears
Extinction Events	Endings, rebirth, profound change	Ritual themes for releasing and renewal

Integrating Shadow Aspects
Shadow work is not about eliminating parts of ourselves but integrating them harmoniously.
1. Acceptance

- Acknowledge that all aspects of yourself serve a purpose.
- Practice self-compassion and avoid self-judgment.

2. Expression

- Find healthy outlets for shadow aspects (e.g., art, writing, physical activity).
- Use creative expression to explore and process emotions.

3. Boundaries

- Set boundaries to ensure shadow traits do not harm yourself or others.
- Recognize triggers and develop strategies to manage reactions.

4. Continuous Reflection

- Regularly engage in practices like journaling or meditation to stay connected with your inner world.
- Monitor your growth and celebrate progress.

Safety and Self-Care in Shadow Work

Shadow work can be intense and emotionally challenging. Prioritize self-care:

- **Grounding Techniques:** Use grounding exercises after sessions to stabilize your energy.
- **Professional Support:** Consider seeking guidance from a therapist or counselor, especially when dealing with deep-seated traumas.
- **Rest and Nourishment:** Ensure you get adequate rest, nutrition, and engage in activities that bring joy and relaxation.
- **Set Limits:** If a session becomes overwhelming, it's okay to pause and return to it later.

Enhancing Shadow Work with Prehistoric Magick

1. Use of Sound

- **Drumming:** Mimic the heartbeat of the Earth to enter deeper states of consciousness.
- **Vocalizations:** Use guttural sounds or chants to connect with primal energies.

2. Artistic Expression

- **Drawing or Painting:** Create images of your shadow or prehistoric symbols.
- **Sculpting:** Mold clay or other materials into representations of shadow aspects.

3. Ritual Movement

- **Dance:** Move intuitively to embody the energy of prehistoric creatures.
- **Postures:** Adopt poses that reflect the strength or vulnerability you're exploring.

Benefits of Prehistoric Shadow Work

- **Empowerment:** Transform fears into sources of strength.
- **Authenticity:** Live more genuinely by embracing all parts of yourself.
- **Enhanced Magickal Abilities:** Clear inner blocks to amplify your magickal practice.
- **Deeper Understanding:** Gain profound insights into your behaviors and patterns.

Closing Reflections

Prehistoric shadow work is a journey into the depths of your being, guided by the ancient energies of the Earth and its earliest inhabitants. By confronting and embracing your inner shadows, you unlock the potential for profound healing, growth, and transformation. This practice is not about dwelling in darkness but about bringing light to the unseen parts of yourself, integrating them into a harmonious whole.

As you delve into this work, remember that you are supported by the primal forces that have shaped existence for millennia. Let the strength, resilience, and wisdom of the prehistoric world empower you on your path toward self-discovery and magickal mastery.

Continue your exploration of **The Dino Grimoire**, carrying forward the insights and growth you've gained, and embracing the fullness of your magickal potential.

Chapter 31: Dinosaur Migration Spells

Migration is a universal phenomenon that signifies movement, adaptation, and survival. In the prehistoric world, dinosaurs embarked on vast migrations, traversing continents in search of food, water, and favorable conditions. These journeys, dictated by instinct and environmental cycles, symbolize resilience, guidance, and the ability to navigate life's transitions. By drawing inspiration from these ancient migration patterns, you can create spells and rituals to help navigate your own life transitions—whether they involve personal growth, career changes, relationships, or spiritual evolution.

This chapter delves into the symbolism of dinosaur migrations, provides rituals and spells inspired by their patterns, and explores how these ancient movements can guide your magickal practice.

The Symbolism of Dinosaur Migrations

Dinosaur migrations were monumental undertakings that required coordination, instinct, and adaptation. These movements carry profound magickal symbolism:

1. **Transition and Change:** Migrations represent leaving behind the old to embrace the new.
2. **Instinct and Guidance:** Following internal and external cues to navigate unknown paths.
3. **Resilience:** Overcoming obstacles and enduring challenges to reach the destination.
4. **Community and Cooperation:** Working together to achieve shared goals.
5. **Cycles and Renewal:** Aligning with natural rhythms, such as seasonal changes or life stages.

Dinosaurs and Their Migration Patterns

Understanding the migration habits of specific dinosaurs can enhance your connection to their energy in your spells:

1. **Hadrosaurs (Duck-Billed Dinosaurs):** Known for their long-distance migrations, they symbolize perseverance and the ability to adapt to environmental shifts.
2. **Sauropods (Brachiosaurus, Diplodocus):** These massive herbivores migrated in search of food and water, embodying endurance and stability during transitions.
3. **Ceratopsians (Triceratops):** Traveling in herds for protection and sustenance, they symbolize safety and unity during life changes.
4. **Theropods (Tyrannosaurus Rex, Velociraptor):** Smaller groups of predators often followed migrating herds, representing strategic movement and precision.

Preparing for Migration Spells

To perform effective migration spells, prepare yourself and your environment:

1. Define Your Transition

Identify the life transition you're navigating, such as a career change, relationship shift, or spiritual transformation.

2. Gather Symbolic Tools

Incorporate items that align with migration and dinosaur energy:

- **Fossils or Stones:** Use fossils of migrating dinosaurs (e.g., hadrosaur fossils) or crystals like labradorite (transformation) and malachite (growth).
- **Candles:** Green for growth, blue for clarity, or white for guidance.
- **Herbs and Scents:** Sage (cleansing), rosemary (memory and guidance), and lavender (calm transitions).
- **Symbols of Movement:** Feathers, footprints, or maps.

3. Create a Sacred Space

Cleanse your ritual area with smoke, sound, or salt water. Arrange your tools on an altar or workspace, incorporating elements of movement and change, such as flowing water or spirals.

Dinosaur Migration Spells

1. Pathfinding Spell

Purpose: Find clarity and direction during times of uncertainty.

Materials Needed:

- A piece of malachite or fossilized tooth (symbolizing guidance).
- A green candle.
- A map or symbolic representation of a path (drawn or printed).

Steps:

1. Light the green candle and place the malachite or fossil at the center of the map.
2. Close your eyes and visualize yourself as a dinosaur in a vast landscape, searching for the right path.
3. Chant:
   "Ancient travelers, strong and wise,
   Show me the path where my future lies.
   Through shifting winds and changing ground,
   Guide my steps where hope is found."

4. Allow your intuition to guide you as you trace your fingers over the map. Pause when you feel drawn to a specific spot or direction.
5. Reflect on the area or symbol you're drawn to and how it relates to your situation.

2. Resilience Ritual
Purpose: Strengthen your endurance and resolve during difficult transitions.
Materials Needed:

- A piece of petrified wood or dinosaur bone.
- A white candle.
- A bowl of water.

Steps:

1. Light the white candle and hold the petrified wood or bone in your hand.
2. Visualize yourself as a Sauropod, moving steadily through a prehistoric landscape. Feel your strength and determination.
3. Chant:
   "Like Sauropods on a timeless quest,
   I move forward, I do my best.
   Resilient and strong, I press ahead,
   With ancient wisdom, my fears are shed."
4. Dip your fingers into the water and touch your forehead, symbolizing clarity and endurance.
5. Carry the petrified wood or bone with you as a talisman of resilience.

3. Unity Spell
Purpose: Foster cooperation and support during group transitions or shared challenges.
Materials Needed:

- A piece of fluorite (symbolizing harmony).
- A blue candle.
- A circle of small stones or tokens to represent each person involved.

Steps:

1. Place the fluorite at the center of the circle, with the stones or tokens around it.
2. Light the blue candle and visualize the group as a herd of Triceratops, moving together with strength and unity.
3. Chant:
   "Together we move, strong and aligned,
   Through every challenge, our strength combined.

In unity and trust, we find our way,
Supporting each other every day."
4. Keep the fluorite on your altar as a reminder of collective strength.

4. Cycle Renewal Spell
Purpose: Embrace the end of one cycle and the beginning of another.
Materials Needed:

- A piece of ammonite fossil.
- A black candle (for endings) and a green candle (for beginnings).
- A small journal or paper for writing reflections.

Steps:

1. Light the black candle, holding the ammonite fossil in your hand.
2. Write down what you are leaving behind and reflect on the lessons learned.
3. Chant:
   "As cycles end, new ones begin,
   Through ancient tides, I find within.
   From past to future, I carry the flame,
   Renewed in spirit, never the same."
4. Extinguish the black candle and light the green candle, symbolizing new beginnings.
5. Write down your intentions for the next phase and place the ammonite fossil on top as a focus point.

Meditative Practices for Migration Energy
1. Footprint Visualization

- Close your eyes and visualize dinosaur footprints stretching before you.
- Imagine yourself stepping into each print, guided by the wisdom and energy of ancient travelers.

2. Herd Movement Meditation

- Visualize yourself as part of a dinosaur herd, moving together across a vast landscape.
- Feel the strength and support of the group as you navigate challenges together.

Daily Practices for Navigating Transitions

1. **Carry Fossils or Stones:** Keep a fossil or migration-aligned stone with you as a talisman of guidance and resilience.
2. **Symbolic Movement:** Take daily walks or engage in physical movement to symbolize forward momentum.
3. **Journaling:** Record your progress, insights, and emotions during transitions.

Magickal Benefits of Dinosaur Migration Spells

- **Clarity and Direction:** Gain insight into your path and purpose.
- **Strength and Resilience:** Draw on the endurance of migrating dinosaurs to overcome obstacles.
- **Support and Unity:** Foster cooperation and harmony in group dynamics.
- **Adaptability and Growth:** Embrace change with confidence and grace.

Closing Thoughts on Migration Spells

Dinosaur migration spells embody the spirit of movement, transformation, and survival. By aligning with the instincts and resilience of these ancient creatures, you can navigate life's transitions with strength, clarity, and purpose. Whether you're embarking on a new journey, seeking support, or letting go of the past, these rituals offer guidance and empowerment.

Let the enduring wisdom of prehistoric migrations guide your path as you continue your journey through **The Dino Grimoire**, transforming life's challenges into opportunities for growth and renewal.

Chapter 32: Taming the Chaos of Extinction

Extinction events are dramatic, transformative occurrences that have shaped Earth's history, wiping out species while paving the way for new life. These cataclysmic moments of destruction are not merely endings but are also opportunities for profound renewal and rebirth. In prehistoric times, extinction events such as the asteroid that ended the age of dinosaurs symbolize the inevitability of change and the resilience of life. Taming the chaos of extinction in your magickal practice involves transforming these powerful energies of upheaval into forces of growth, healing, and renewal.

This chapter explores the magickal symbolism of extinction events, their role in prehistoric history, and rituals to channel their transformative power for personal and spiritual evolution.

The Magickal Symbolism of Extinction Events

Extinction events hold deep spiritual and magickal significance:

1. **Endings and Beginnings:** Extinction represents the end of one phase, making space for something new to emerge.
2. **Chaos and Order:** The destructive chaos of extinction can be harnessed to create balance and renewal.
3. **Cycles of Life:** These events remind us of the cyclical nature of existence—birth, death, and rebirth.
4. **Resilience and Adaptation:** Life's ability to adapt and thrive after mass extinctions embodies strength and endurance.

Prehistoric Extinction Events

Major prehistoric extinction events are steeped in symbolism and provide inspiration for magickal practices:

1. **The Permian-Triassic Extinction ("The Great Dying")**
   - Wiped out approximately 90% of Earth's species.
   - Symbolizes profound endings and the resilience of life in the face of overwhelming odds.
2. **The Cretaceous-Paleogene Extinction**
   - Marked the end of the dinosaurs and the rise of mammals.
   - Represents dramatic transformation and the emergence of new opportunities after destruction.
3. **Smaller Extinction Events**
   - Highlight the importance of adaptation, resourcefulness, and survival in the face of change.

Magickal Correspondences for Extinction Energy

Aspect	Symbolism	Magickal Uses
Asteroids/Comets	Sudden change, cosmic power	Transformation, releasing stagnation
Volcanic Eruptions	Chaos, cleansing, renewal	Purification, creating fertile energy
Fossils	Endurance, wisdom	Grounding, tapping into ancient strength
Ashes	Fertility, rebirth	Releasing the past, nurturing growth

Preparing for Extinction Energy Work

1. Define Your Purpose

What aspect of your life needs transformation? Examples include releasing old habits, ending toxic relationships, or embracing personal growth.

2. Gather Tools

Use materials that symbolize endings, destruction, and rebirth:

- **Fossils:** Representing the wisdom of what remains after endings.
- **Ashes or Charcoal:** Symbolizing destruction and fertility.
- **Crystals:**
    - **Obsidian:** For protection and transformation.
    - **Labradorite:** For embracing change.
    - **Smoky Quartz:** For grounding during upheaval.
- **Candles:** Black for endings, white for new beginnings.

3. Create a Sacred Space

Prepare your ritual area by cleansing it with sage or salt water. Arrange your tools on an altar, incorporating elements that represent destruction and renewal (e.g., lava rocks, feathers, or seeds).

Rituals for Taming Extinction Energy
1. The Extinction and Rebirth Ritual
Purpose: Release what no longer serves you and embrace renewal.
Materials Needed:

- A black candle and a white candle.
- A fossil or stone (symbolizing resilience).
- A piece of paper and pen.
- A fire-safe bowl.

Steps:

1. Light the black candle and reflect on what you need to release. Write these aspects on the paper.
2. Hold the fossil or stone and visualize yourself in the chaos of an extinction event—imagine destructive forces clearing away the old.
3. Chant:
   "Chaos of old, destruction pure,
   End what was, let renewal endure.
   Through endings fierce, life shall arise,
   From ashes dark, new light flies."
4. Burn the paper in the black candle's flame, letting go of what no longer serves you.
5. Light the white candle and visualize the emergence of new energy and opportunities.
6. Place the fossil on your altar as a reminder of resilience and growth.

2. Cosmic Transformation Spell

Purpose: Harness the energy of meteoric impacts to catalyze transformation.
Materials Needed:

- A piece of tektite or obsidian.
- A silver or dark blue candle.
- A small mirror or reflective surface.

Steps:

1. Light the candle and place the tektite or obsidian on the mirror.
2. Visualize a meteor striking the Earth, releasing an explosion of energy that clears away old patterns.
3. Chant:
   "Meteor bright, with cosmic might,
   Break through darkness, bring new light.
   Transform my path, ignite my core,
   Let me rise, renewed once more."
4. Hold the tektite and visualize your personal transformation taking shape.

3. Fertility from Ashes Ritual

Purpose: Use the energy of destruction to nurture new growth and opportunities.
Materials Needed:

- A handful of ash or soil.
- Seeds or a small plant.
- A green candle.

Steps:

1. Light the green candle and hold the ash in your hand. Reflect on the cycles of destruction and renewal.
2. Sprinkle the ash into the soil as you plant the seeds or place the plant in its new home.
3. Chant:
   "From ash to soil, life is sown,
   Through ancient cycles, I have grown.
   Renewal springs, strong and free,
   Fertile ground, so mote it be."

4. Care for the plant as a symbol of your transformation.

Meditative Practices for Extinction Energy
1. Ashes to Light Visualization

- Sit quietly with a black candle.
- Visualize yourself surrounded by ashes, remnants of an old phase.
- Imagine light emerging from the ashes, illuminating new possibilities.

2. Fossil Reflection Meditation

- Hold a fossil in your hand.
- Meditate on its journey through time, surviving mass extinction and transformation.
- Reflect on your own resilience and ability to adapt.

Daily Practices for Embracing Extinction Energy

1. **Carry a Talisman:** Keep a fossil or extinction-aligned stone as a reminder of resilience and renewal.
2. **Daily Affirmations:** Use phrases like:
    ◦ "From endings, I rise renewed."
    ◦ "Chaos brings clarity and growth."
3. **Journal Your Transformation:** Write about old patterns you've released and the new opportunities you're embracing.

Magickal Benefits of Extinction Energy

- **Personal Growth:** Transform challenges into opportunities for self-improvement.
- **Renewed Purpose:** Gain clarity and direction by releasing the old.
- **Strength and Resilience:** Build inner strength by confronting and overcoming chaos.
- **Alignment with Cycles:** Embrace the natural rhythms of endings and beginnings.

Closing Reflections on Extinction Magick

Taming the chaos of extinction is a transformative practice that helps you embrace the cycles of life, death, and rebirth. By channeling the energy of prehistoric extinction events, you can turn destruction into a catalyst for renewal, growth, and empowerment. These rituals and meditations allow you to navigate life's upheavals with grace, strength, and resilience, honoring the primal forces that shaped our world.

Let the wisdom of extinction guide your magickal journey as you continue to explore **The Dino Grimoire**, transforming chaos into creation and challenges into triumphs.

Chapter 33: Summoning the Dino Guardian Spirits

The prehistoric world was alive with powerful creatures, many of which embodied unique traits of strength, resilience, and wisdom. These ancient beings, now long extinct, have left behind energetic echoes that can be tapped into by those seeking protection, guidance, and spiritual support. Dino guardian spirits are archetypal energies or astral entities linked to specific dinosaur species, each offering their unique strengths and qualities. Through rituals and invocations, you can summon these guardian spirits to act as protectors, guides, and sources of ancient wisdom.

This chapter provides a comprehensive guide to understanding, summoning, and working with Dino guardian spirits, detailing their symbolism, attributes, and methods of connection.

The Role of Dino Guardian Spirits

Guardian spirits serve as protectors, guides, and allies in your magickal journey. Dino guardian spirits are no different, embodying the primal power, wisdom, and adaptability of their prehistoric counterparts. They can assist with:

1. **Protection:** Shielding you from negative energies or harm.
2. **Guidance:** Offering insight and wisdom during challenging times.
3. **Empowerment:** Instilling confidence, resilience, and courage.
4. **Spiritual Connection:** Deepening your bond with the Earth's ancient energies.

Symbolism of Dino Guardian Spirits

Each dinosaur species carries unique symbolism, which informs its role as a guardian spirit:

1. Tyrannosaurus Rex (The Protector)

- **Symbolism:** Strength, authority, and fearlessness.
- **Attributes:** Instills courage, protects against threats, and empowers you to stand your ground.
- **Best For:** Overcoming fear, asserting dominance, and personal empowerment.

2. Triceratops (The Defender)

- **Symbolism:** Defense, stability, and community.
- **Attributes:** Shields against negative energies, fortifies boundaries, and promotes group harmony.
- **Best For:** Protection, creating safe spaces, and maintaining balance in relationships.

3. Velociraptor (The Strategist)

- **Symbolism:** Agility, intelligence, and cunning.
- **Attributes:** Provides strategic insight, quick thinking, and adaptability.
- **Best For:** Problem-solving, making decisive choices, and achieving goals.

4. Brachiosaurus (The Guardian of Growth)

- **Symbolism:** Endurance, patience, and steady progress.
- **Attributes:** Promotes long-term planning, emotional resilience, and personal growth.
- **Best For:** Overcoming obstacles, fostering patience, and nurturing success.

5. Pterodactyl (The Watcher)

- **Symbolism:** Perspective, freedom, and spiritual elevation.
- **Attributes:** Helps gain clarity, see the bigger picture, and rise above challenges.
- **Best For:** Introspection, spiritual awakening, and navigating life transitions.

Preparing to Summon Dino Guardian Spirits
1. Set Your Intention
Identify the purpose of summoning the guardian spirit. Examples include protection, guidance, or empowerment.
2. Create a Sacred Space
Prepare an environment conducive to summoning rituals:

- **Cleanse the Space:** Use sage, palo santo, or sound cleansing to clear negative energy.
- **Arrange an Altar:** Include fossils, dinosaur figurines, candles, and other prehistoric symbols.
- **Choose the Right Tools:** Match your tools to the spirit you wish to summon (e.g., black candles for protection, green for growth).

3. Gather Materials

- **Fossils or Stones:** Choose fossils or crystals that align with the spirit's energy (e.g., petrified wood for Brachiosaurus, obsidian for Tyrannosaurus Rex).
- **Candles:** Color-coded to the spirit's attributes.
- **Incense or Oils:** Scents like cedarwood, pine, or frankincense evoke ancient Earth energies.
- **Symbols or Drawings:** Create or print an image of the dinosaur to act as a focus.

Rituals to Summon Dino Guardian Spirits
1. Invocation of the Tyrannosaurus Rex
Purpose: Call upon the T-Rex for strength, protection, and dominance.
Materials Needed:

- A black or red candle.
- A piece of obsidian or tiger's eye.
- A dinosaur tooth or sharp object (symbolizing strength).

Steps:

1. Light the candle and place the obsidian or tiger's eye in front of you.
2. Focus on the image or energy of the T-Rex, visualizing it towering over you, its presence fierce and protective.
3. Chant:
   "Mighty Rex, protector bold,
   Your strength and power I now behold.
   Shield my spirit, guide my might,
   Stand with me through darkest night."
4. Feel the T-Rex's energy surrounding you, filling you with courage and resolve.
5. Thank the spirit and extinguish the candle, leaving the stone on your altar for ongoing connection.

2. Summoning the Triceratops
Purpose: Invoke the Triceratops for protection, stability, and community harmony.
Materials Needed:

- A green candle.
- A piece of jade or malachite.
- A symbolic shield or small circle of stones.

Steps:

1. Light the green candle and arrange the stones in a circle around you.
2. Visualize the Triceratops standing guard, its horns and frill forming a protective barrier.
3. Chant:
   "Defender strong, with shield and horn,
   Protect my space, where peace is born.

Triceratops, your strength I claim,
Guard my path, in your name."

4. Imagine the protective barrier strengthening around you, ensuring safety and balance.

3. Invoking the Velociraptor

Purpose: Call upon the Velociraptor for agility, strategy, and quick thinking.

Materials Needed:

- A yellow or orange candle.
- A sharp crystal (e.g., quartz or citrine).
- A feather or lightweight object.

Steps:

1. Light the candle and hold the crystal, focusing on the Velociraptor's energy—swift, clever, and strategic.
2. Chant:
   "Swift Raptor, sharp and keen,
   Guide my steps, clear and clean.
   Show the path, the moves to make,
   Your cunning wisdom I awake."
3. Visualize yourself embodying the Velociraptor's agility and intelligence, moving through challenges with ease.

4. Calling the Brachiosaurus

Purpose: Summon the Brachiosaurus for endurance, growth, and stability.

Materials Needed:

- A green or brown candle.
- A piece of petrified wood or a grounding stone like smoky quartz.
- A small potted plant or seed.

Steps:

1. Light the candle and hold the petrified wood, grounding yourself in its steady energy.
2. Chant:
   "Gentle giant, tall and wise,
   Steady growth beneath wide skies.
   Teach me patience, enduring grace,
   Guide my steps at life's slow pace."
3. Plant the seed or tend to the plant as a symbol of the growth and resilience you're fostering.

5. Invoking the Pterodactyl
Purpose: Connect with the Pterodactyl for perspective, clarity, and spiritual freedom.
Materials Needed:

- A blue or white candle.
- A piece of lapis lazuli or amethyst.
- A small wing-shaped object or feather.

Steps:

1. Light the candle and place the lapis lazuli or amethyst before you.
2. Visualize the Pterodactyl soaring above a vast landscape, its view offering clarity and insight.
3. Chant:
   "Sky-borne watcher, spirit free,
   Lift my sight, let wisdom be.
   Through your wings, my spirit flies,
   Show me truth beyond the skies."
4. Spend a few moments meditating on the messages or insights the Pterodactyl offers.

Daily Practices to Connect with Dino Guardian Spirits

1. **Wear a Talisman:** Carry a fossil or stone linked to your chosen guardian spirit for ongoing connection.
2. **Meditate Daily:** Spend a few minutes visualizing the spirit's presence and guidance.
3. **Offer Gratitude:** Leave small offerings on your altar, such as plants, seeds, or symbolic objects.
4. **Journal Experiences:** Record any dreams, synchronicities, or insights you receive from working with the spirit.

Magickal Benefits of Dino Guardian Spirits

- **Protection:** Shield yourself from negativity and harm with the power of ancient protectors.
- **Guidance:** Receive wisdom and clarity during times of uncertainty.
- **Empowerment:** Strengthen your resolve and confidence by channeling primal energies.
- **Spiritual Connection:** Deepen your relationship with Earth's ancient forces and cycles.

Closing Reflections

Summoning Dino guardian spirits allows you to draw on the strength, wisdom, and resilience of Earth's prehistoric giants. These spirits offer powerful support, whether you seek protection, guidance, or empowerment. By building a relationship with these ancient energies, you honor the legacy of the prehistoric world while enhancing your magickal journey.

Let these guardians stand beside you as you explore **The Dino Grimoire**, guiding and protecting you with their timeless strength and wisdom.

Chapter 34: The Magick of Prehistoric Sound

Sound has been a vital force in the history of life, shaping communication, connection, and survival. In the prehistoric world, dinosaurs communicated through a range of sounds, from deep resonant calls to high-pitched cries, creating a soundscape as ancient as the Earth itself. These primal vibrations can be invoked in modern magick to amplify intentions, deepen meditative states, and connect with the ancient energies of the prehistoric world.

This chapter explores the magickal significance of sound, the possible calls of dinosaurs, and practical methods to incorporate these sounds into chanting, rituals, and spiritual practices.

The Magickal Power of Sound

Sound is a fundamental force in magick, carrying energy and intention through vibration. Its magickal significance includes:

1. **Manifestation:** Vibrations help align intentions with the universe.
2. **Healing:** Sound clears energetic blockages and promotes balance.
3. **Connection:** Calls and chants create bonds between the practitioner and spiritual realms.
4. **Focus and Amplification:** Chanting sharpens concentration and intensifies rituals.

Prehistoric Soundscapes

The prehistoric world was alive with sound, as dinosaurs and other ancient creatures communicated and interacted. While the exact sounds made by dinosaurs cannot be confirmed, paleontologists hypothesize that they used a variety of vocalizations, including:

1. **Low-Frequency Rumbles:** Large dinosaurs like Brachiosaurus likely produced deep rumbles that traveled long distances.
2. **Trumpeting Calls:** Dinosaurs with crests, such as Parasaurolophus, may have used their hollow crests to create resonant, trumpet-like sounds.
3. **Growls and Roars:** Carnivorous dinosaurs like Tyrannosaurus Rex likely used growls or roars to intimidate rivals or assert dominance.
4. **High-Pitched Cries:** Smaller dinosaurs like Velociraptors may have used chirps, squawks, or shrieks for communication within packs.

These sounds were not only functional but also carried energy and intent, making them potent tools for magickal practice.

Symbolism of Prehistoric Sounds

Each type of sound holds specific symbolism and magickal applications:

Sound Type	Symbolism	Magickal Uses
Low-Frequency Rumbles	Stability, grounding	Grounding rituals, connecting to Earth energy.
Trumpeting Calls	Communication, clarity	Chanting for truth, connecting with higher realms.
Growls and Roars	Strength, dominance	Protection spells, asserting personal power.
High-Pitched Cries	Alertness, agility	Focus, quick decision-making, enhancing intuition.

Incorporating Prehistoric Sound in Magick
1. Chanting and Vocalization
Recreate the essence of prehistoric calls through chanting and vocal exercises:

- **Low Tones:** Mimic the grounding rumbles of large dinosaurs by chanting deep, resonant tones like "Om" or humming.
- **Crest Sounds:** Use long, drawn-out vowels (e.g., "Oooo" or "Eeee") to mimic the trumpet-like calls of crested dinosaurs.
- **Roars and Growls:** Channel your inner T-Rex by vocalizing growls or roars to release energy or build power.
- **Quick Chirps:** Use high-pitched sounds or repeated syllables like "Tsi-Tsi-Tsi" for agility and focus.

2. Instruments Inspired by Prehistoric Sounds
Incorporate instruments to amplify the effects of prehistoric sound magick:

- **Drums:** Create low, rhythmic beats to replicate dinosaur footfalls or heartbeats, grounding your energy.
- **Didgeridoos or Horns:** Use these for deep, resonant tones akin to the rumbles of sauropods.
- **Wind Chimes or Flutes:** Mimic high-pitched cries or calls, invoking clarity and alertness.
- **Rattles:** Represent the quick, sharp sounds of smaller dinosaurs, adding an element of urgency and focus to rituals.

3. Visualization with Prehistoric Sound
Combine sound with visualization to enhance its magickal effects:

1. **Grounding with Rumbles:**
   - Chant or hum a deep tone, visualizing roots extending from your feet into the Earth, connecting with its ancient energy.
2. **Manifestation with Trumpeting Calls:**
   - Blow into a horn or chant loudly, visualizing your intention traveling outward like sound waves, manifesting your desires.
3. **Protection with Roars:**
   - Vocalize a strong roar, imagining a protective barrier forming around you, intimidating negative energies or entities.
4. **Focus with Chirps:**
   - Make quick, high-pitched sounds while visualizing sharp, clear thoughts and swift action.

Rituals Using Prehistoric Sound
1. Grounding Ritual: The Brachiosaurus's Call
Purpose: Connect with Earth's ancient energy for grounding and stability.
Materials Needed:

- A drum or low-pitched instrument (optional).
- A piece of petrified wood or basalt.

Steps:

1. Sit comfortably with the petrified wood or basalt in your hand.
2. Begin humming or drumming a slow, deep rhythm, mimicking the low-frequency rumbles of a Brachiosaurus.
3. Chant:
   "From ancient Earth, vibrations low,
   Root my spirit, let strength grow.
   Through timeless sound, I find my place,
   Grounded deep in nature's grace."
4. Visualize yourself becoming one with the Earth, stable and strong.

2. Manifestation Ritual: The Parasaurolophus Trumpet
Purpose: Amplify your intention and send it into the universe.
Materials Needed:

- A horn or wind instrument (optional).
- A clear quartz crystal.

Steps:

1. Hold the quartz crystal and focus on your intention.
2. Blow into the instrument or chant a long, resonant tone, mimicking the trumpet-like call of Parasaurolophus.
3. Chant:
   "Ancient call, strong and true,
   Carry my will, let it break through.
   Echo far, intention rise,
   Manifest beneath the skies."
4. Visualize your intention traveling outward with the sound waves, reaching its target.

3. Protection Ritual: The T-Rex Roar
Purpose: Create a shield of power and intimidate negativity.
Materials Needed:

- A black candle.
- A piece of obsidian or onyx.

Steps:

1. Light the black candle and hold the obsidian in your hand.
2. Take a deep breath and vocalize a strong, guttural roar, imagining the sound creating a protective barrier around you.
3. Chant:
   "Mighty roar, fierce and loud,
   Shield me now in your shroud.
   No harm may pass, no dark may stay,
   Protection strong, night and day."
4. Visualize the barrier solidifying, leaving you surrounded by strength and safety.

4. Focus Ritual: The Velociraptor's Cry
Purpose: Enhance focus and quick decision-making.
Materials Needed:

- A yellow or orange candle.
- A small bell or chime.

Steps:

1. Light the candle and place the bell or chime nearby.
2. Ring the bell or chime sharply, mimicking the high-pitched cries of a Velociraptor.
3. Chant:
   "Quick of mind, sharp of sight,
   Velociraptor, guide my light.
   Help me see, decisions clear,
   Focus strong, no doubt or fear."
4. Visualize clarity and agility as you move through challenges with ease.

Daily Practices with Prehistoric Sound

1. **Morning Grounding Chant:** Begin your day with a low hum or chant to connect with the Earth's energy.
2. **Affirmation Calls:** Vocalize affirmations with resonant tones to empower your intentions.
3. **Meditative Soundscapes:** Use instruments or recordings to create prehistoric soundscapes for meditation and visualization.
4. **Protection Roars:** Practice vocalizing a protective roar when you feel vulnerable or overwhelmed.

Magickal Benefits of Prehistoric Sound

- **Deepened Connection:** Sound bridges the gap between ancient energies and modern practice.
- **Enhanced Ritual Power:** Vibrations amplify the energy of intentions and spells.
- **Healing and Balance:** Sound harmonizes the mind, body, and spirit.
- **Empowerment:** Vocalizing primal sounds builds confidence and strengthens your presence.

Closing Reflections on Prehistoric Sound

The magick of prehistoric sound channels the raw, primal energy of the ancient world, infusing your rituals and practices with vibration, intent, and power. Whether through chanting, instruments, or visualization, these sounds awaken your connection to the Earth's earliest forces, empowering your magickal journey.

As you explore **The Dino Grimoire**, let the echoes of prehistoric calls guide your voice and intentions, amplifying your connection to the timeless energies of the past.

Chapter 35: Living Magick: Keeping the Dino Spirit Alive

Prehistoric magick isn't just about rituals and spells—it's a way of life, a connection to Earth's ancient energies that can shape how you interact with the world. Keeping the Dino spirit alive means embracing the lessons, strengths, and wisdom of these ancient creatures in your daily life. This chapter offers practical advice on integrating prehistoric magick into everyday practices, ensuring that the primal power of the dinosaurs remains a living, guiding force in your magickal journey.

The Core Principles of Living Dino Magick

To integrate prehistoric magick into daily life, focus on these foundational principles:

1. **Connection to Earth's Energy:** Maintain a grounded relationship with nature and its cycles, inspired by the dinosaurs' resilience and adaptability.
2. **Embody Primal Strength:** Channel the traits of dinosaurs—courage, strategy, patience, and endurance—in your actions and decisions.
3. **Mindfulness in Practice:** Recognize magick in everyday moments, from a walk in nature to setting intentions for the day.
4. **Symbolic Living:** Incorporate dinosaur-inspired symbols, tools, and rituals into your daily routines.

Daily Practices to Keep the Dino Spirit Alive
1. Morning Grounding Ritual
Begin your day by grounding yourself with Earth's ancient energy:
Steps:

1. Sit in a quiet space with a fossil, stone, or grounding crystal (e.g., petrified wood, smoky quartz).
2. Close your eyes and visualize roots growing from your feet into the Earth, connecting to the primal energy of prehistoric times.
3. Chant softly:
   "From ancient Earth, my strength is drawn,
   Dino spirit, with me at dawn.
   Guide my steps, bold and true,
   Grounded deeply, I renew."

2. Dino Spirit Affirmations
Incorporate affirmations inspired by dinosaurs' traits to set positive intentions for the day. Examples:

- **Strength (T-Rex):** "I stand strong and fearless, ready to face any challenge."
- **Patience (Brachiosaurus):** "I move with steady purpose, embracing growth at my own pace."
- **Agility (Velociraptor):** "I adapt quickly and navigate life's challenges with precision."
- **Protection (Triceratops):** "I am surrounded by a shield of safety and balance."

Repeat these affirmations while holding a fossil or dinosaur symbol for added focus.
3. Magickal Journaling
Keep a journal to document your connection with Dino magick. Suggested entries:

- Reflect on how dinosaur traits can guide you in specific situations.
- Write dreams or meditations involving prehistoric imagery.
- Record daily intentions or rituals inspired by Dino energy.

4. Symbolic Jewelry and Talismans
Wear or carry items that represent your connection to Dino magick:

- **Fossil Jewelry:** Ammonites, amber, or petrified wood pieces to embody Earth's ancient power.
- **Crystal Talismans:** Use crystals like obsidian (protection), citrine (manifestation), or labradorite (transformation).

- **Dinosaur Figurines or Symbols:** Carry a small token of your guardian dinosaur spirit for ongoing guidance.

5. Prehistoric Movement Meditation

Incorporate dinosaur-inspired movements into your meditative practice to embody their energy physically:

- **T-Rex Stance:** Stand firmly with wide, grounded feet and visualize strength radiating from your core.
- **Brachiosaurus Stretch:** Stretch your arms upward, mimicking the reach of a Brachiosaurus feeding on tall trees, focusing on growth and expansion.
- **Velociraptor Flow:** Move swiftly and deliberately in short, sharp motions, embodying agility and precision.

Incorporating Dino Magick in Rituals and Celebrations
1. Seasonal Celebrations

Align your magickal practice with Earth's cycles, as dinosaurs did with their migrations and habits:

- **Spring (Renewal):** Honor the emergence of life with rituals for growth and new beginnings, invoking the energy of herbivorous dinosaurs like Hadrosaurs.
- **Summer (Strength):** Channel the dominance and vitality of the T-Rex to amplify your personal power and confidence.
- **Autumn (Transformation):** Reflect on change and resilience, inspired by dinosaurs that adapted to shifting environments.
- **Winter (Introspection):** Meditate on the mysteries of extinction and renewal, using fossils as focal points.

2. Personal Milestones
Celebrate life transitions with Dino magick:

- **New Beginnings:** Invoke the Parasaurolophus for guidance in exploring new opportunities.
- **Endings and Letting Go:** Perform extinction-inspired rituals to release old patterns and embrace rebirth.
- **Achievements:** Honor success with a gratitude ritual, calling upon the resilience of the Triceratops or the patience of the Brachiosaurus.

Infusing Dino Magick into Your Environment
1. Create a Dino Altar
Maintain a dedicated space to honor prehistoric energies. Include:

- Fossils and stones representing specific dinosaurs.
- Candles in colors aligned with your intentions (e.g., green for growth, red for strength).
- Dinosaur figurines or drawings.
- Fresh plants, soil, or water to connect with Earth's primal elements.

2. Home Decor
Incorporate prehistoric themes into your living space:

- **Fossil Art:** Display fossils or replicas to keep Dino energy present.
- **Natural Elements:** Use earthy tones, stones, and wooden accents to reflect ancient landscapes.
- **Dinosaur Motifs:** Integrate subtle dinosaur patterns or symbols into textiles, artwork, or jewelry.

Modern Applications of Dino Wisdom
1. Decision-Making
Approach decisions with the traits of your chosen Dino guardian spirit:

- **T-Rex:** Be bold and decisive.
- **Velociraptor:** Strategize and adapt quickly.
- **Brachiosaurus:** Take your time, ensuring steady, thoughtful progress.

2. Relationships
Use Dino-inspired qualities to enhance interactions:

- **Triceratops:** Promote harmony and protect boundaries.
- **Parasaurolophus:** Improve communication and connection with others.

3. Career and Creativity
Channel Dino energy to overcome challenges and achieve goals:

- **T-Rex:** Assert leadership and tackle obstacles head-on.
- **Pterodactyl:** Seek new perspectives and think outside the box.

Maintaining Your Connection to Dino Magick
1. Regular Reflection
Take time weekly to reflect on how prehistoric magick has influenced your life. Consider questions like:

- What Dino qualities have helped me this week?
- How can I deepen my connection to these energies?
- What lessons can I learn from the prehistoric world?

2. Refresh Rituals and Practices
Adapt your Dino magick as your needs and circumstances evolve:

- Introduce new rituals or chants inspired by different dinosaurs.
- Replace altar items with symbols that reflect your current focus.

3. Share the Wisdom
Share your connection to Dino magick with others by:

- Teaching the symbolism of dinosaurs to friends or coven members.
- Creating artwork, stories, or music inspired by prehistoric energies.
- Hosting group rituals celebrating Dino magick.

Magickal Benefits of Living Dino Magick

- **Empowerment:** Build confidence and resilience by embodying the traits of ancient giants.
- **Grounding:** Maintain a deep connection to Earth's energies through fossils, rituals, and mindfulness.
- **Adaptability:** Navigate life's challenges with the adaptability of prehistoric creatures.
- **Spiritual Growth:** Enhance your spiritual practice with the timeless wisdom of the prehistoric world.

Closing Reflections on Living Dino Magick
Living Dino magick transforms prehistoric wisdom into a practical, daily tool for personal growth, spiritual connection, and empowerment. By keeping the Dino spirit alive, you honor the Earth's ancient history while drawing on its energies to navigate your own journey.

Let this magick guide you as you continue to explore **The Dino Grimoire**, building a life enriched with the strength, resilience, and wisdom of the prehistoric past.

Appendices

Appendix A: Prehistoric Correspondences

This appendix serves as a reference guide for dinosaurs, their symbolic meanings, and their associated magickal attributes. By understanding the unique qualities of each dinosaur, you can align your intentions and magickal practices with their energy, channeling the ancient power of the prehistoric world.

Prehistoric Correspondences Table

Dinosaur	Symbolic Meaning	Magickal Attributes	Ideal Uses in Magick
Tyrannosaurus Rex	Strength, dominance, fearlessness	Protection, empowerment, courage	Protection spells, overcoming fear, asserting authority
Triceratops	Defense, stability, community	Shielding, grounding, fostering harmony	Creating safe spaces, strengthening relationships, warding off negativity
Velociraptor	Agility, strategy, quick thinking	Focus, precision, adaptability	Problem-solving, decision-making, achieving goals
Brachiosaurus	Endurance, patience, growth	Long-term planning, emotional resilience, steady progress	Overcoming obstacles, fostering patience, nurturing growth
Pterodactyl	Perspective, freedom, elevation	Spiritual insight, clarity, connection to higher realms	Gaining clarity, astral travel, rising above challenges
Stegosaurus	Protection, resilience, grounding	Spiritual shielding, slow but steady progress	Building resilience, creating boundaries, balancing energies
Parasaurolophus	Communication, adaptability	Enhancing communication, amplifying intentions, emotional expression	Improving relationships, creative expression, community building

Dinosaur	Symbolic Meaning	Magickal Attributes	Ideal Uses in Magick
Ankylosaurus	Defense, fortitude, stability	Protective barriers, strength during hardships	Creating magickal shields, enduring tough situations, emotional fortification
Spinosaurus	Flexibility, water energy, power	Adaptation, duality of strength and flow	Working with water magick, embracing transformation, balancing strength
Carnotaurus	Speed, focus, determination	Goal-oriented action, competitive edge	Achieving victories, sharpening focus, outmaneuvering obstacles
Iguanodon	Resourcefulness, balance	Sustaining energy, adaptability to changing circumstances	Manifestation rituals, balancing priorities, adapting to new environments
Apatosaurus	Wisdom, legacy, grounding energy	Deep connection to Earth, ancestral wisdom, patience	Meditating on ancestral energy, building stability, grounding practices
Allosaurus	Aggression, dominance, courage	Harnessing controlled power, overcoming challenges	Asserting independence, facing fears, fighting injustice
Compsognathus	Quick action, precision, focus	Small but impactful changes, attention to detail	Improving efficiency, making small but powerful moves, precision rituals
Dreadnoughtus	Confidence, strength, presence	Embracing power, resilience, overcoming intimidation	Building self-confidence, enhancing personal presence, achieving bold goals
Diplodocus	Community, cooperation, connection	Working harmoniously with others, gentle strength	Team-building rituals, fostering collaboration, harmonious group dynamics

Dinosaur	Symbolic Meaning	Magickal Attributes	Ideal Uses in Magick
Hadrosaurus	Resilience, adaptability, survival	Endurance through adversity, renewal	Strengthening willpower, enduring challenges, adapting to change
Deinonychus	Alertness, precision, teamwork	Collaboration, sharp focus, tactical thinking	Team-focused efforts, competitive success, detailed planning
Corythosaurus	Creativity, expression, balance	Enhanced creativity, artistic inspiration, emotional balance	Creative pursuits, balancing emotions, amplifying imagination
Pachycephalosaurus	Determination, hard-headedness	Mental resilience, pushing through obstacles	Breaking through barriers, solidifying plans, overcoming doubts
Therizinosaurus	Gentleness, duality, inner strength	Balancing gentleness and ferocity, self-reflection	Shadow work, balancing extremes, spiritual exploration
Megalosaurus	Strength, primal instinct, survival	Tapping into primal instincts, asserting power	Overcoming primal fears, accessing deep courage, survival-oriented magick
Gallimimus	Swiftness, adaptability, lightness	Quick adaptation, fluidity, staying ahead of challenges	Manifesting quick results, adapting to changes, enhancing mobility
Microraptor	Resourcefulness, versatility	Multi-dimensional thinking, spiritual exploration	Versatile magick, astral travel, problem-solving through unconventional means
Oviraptor	Nurturing, resourcefulness, protection	Fertility, emotional healing, protection of loved ones	Fertility rituals, family protection, fostering emotional connections

Dinosaur	Symbolic Meaning	Magickal Attributes	Ideal Uses in Magick
Stygimoloch	Inner strength, breaking barriers	Pushing limits, uncovering hidden truths	Shadow work, breaking through emotional walls, personal breakthroughs
Utahraptor	Strength, agility, leadership	Combining speed with power, leading with wisdom	Leadership rituals, balancing strength with intelligence, achieving balance
Sauropelta	Protection, endurance, grounding	Strengthening defenses, standing firm under pressure	Protection rituals, emotional resilience, physical endurance
Ceratosaurus	Confidence, individuality, boldness	Asserting uniqueness, standing out in a crowd	Personal empowerment, confidence-building rituals, embracing individuality
Troodon	Intelligence, learning, adaptability	Sharpening intellect, curiosity, exploring new possibilities	Study magick, expanding knowledge, opening to new ideas
Archaeopteryx	Transition, evolution, perspective	Navigating transitions, embracing personal growth	Spiritual evolution, rites of passage, embracing change

How to Use This Table

1. **Choose a Dinosaur:** Identify the dinosaur that resonates with your intention or current need. For example, if you're seeking protection, Triceratops or Ankylosaurus might be ideal.
2. **Incorporate Symbols:** Use corresponding fossils, figurines, or visual representations in your rituals.
3. **Meditate on Traits:** Visualize the dinosaur's energy and imagine embodying its traits in your life.
4. **Align with Rituals:** Incorporate these correspondences into specific spells or ceremonies.

Closing Notes on Prehistoric Correspondences

This table offers a practical guide to channeling the energy of dinosaurs in your magickal practices. Each dinosaur brings unique qualities and ancient wisdom, empowering you to harness their strength, resilience, and adaptability. By aligning your intentions with the symbolic and magickal attributes of these prehistoric creatures, you can enrich your practice and deepen your connection to Earth's ancient power.

Appendix B: Dinosaur Fossil Guide

Fossils are physical remnants of prehistoric life, preserving the essence and energy of creatures that once roamed the Earth. These ancient artifacts hold immense power in magick, serving as conduits to the past and tools for spiritual connection. By incorporating fossils into your spellcraft, you can tap into the timeless wisdom, resilience, and primal energy of the prehistoric world.

This guide provides a comprehensive overview of different types of fossils, their meanings, and how to use them effectively in magickal practices.

Understanding Fossils in Magick

Fossils represent transformation, endurance, and the cycles of life and death. Their magickal significance includes:

1. **Ancient Energy:** Fossils carry the essence of the Earth's distant past, making them powerful tools for grounding and connecting to primal energies.
2. **Transformation:** They symbolize evolution, the passage of time, and the ability to adapt and endure.
3. **Wisdom and Memory:** Fossils act as records of the past, offering insights into the lessons and energies of bygone eras.

Types of Fossils and Their Magickal Uses

1. Dinosaur Bones

Description: Fossilized bones are the most recognizable type of dinosaur fossil, often found in fragments or larger preserved skeletons.

Symbolism: Strength, endurance, and grounding.

Magickal Uses:

- **Grounding Spells:** Hold a dinosaur bone fossil during meditation to connect with Earth's ancient stability.
- **Strength and Resilience:** Use in rituals to build physical or emotional strength.
- **Ancestral Connection:** Call upon the wisdom of ancient Earth through fossilized bones.

2. Fossilized Teeth

Description: Teeth from carnivorous or herbivorous dinosaurs, often sharp or serrated, symbolize survival and power.

Symbolism: Protection, ferocity, and primal instincts.

Magickal Uses:

- **Protection:** Place a fossilized tooth on your altar to ward off negativity.
- **Empowerment:** Carry it as a talisman for confidence and strength in challenging situations.
- **Primal Magick:** Use in spells to awaken your inner instincts and connect with primal energies.

3. Fossilized Claws

Description: Fossilized claws represent a dinosaur's physical prowess and ability to defend itself.
Symbolism: Defense, precision, and focus.
Magickal Uses:

- **Sharp Focus:** Meditate with a claw fossil to enhance mental clarity and precision.
- **Protection Spells:** Incorporate it into rituals to create strong spiritual barriers.
- **Manifestation:** Use claws to "grab hold" of opportunities or desires in manifestation magick.

4. Fossilized Eggs

Description: These fossils represent the remains of dinosaur eggs, symbolizing potential and new beginnings.
Symbolism: Fertility, creation, and transformation.
Magickal Uses:

- **Fertility Rituals:** Use egg fossils in rituals to enhance fertility and creative energy.
- **New Beginnings:** Place on your altar during transitions to symbolize rebirth and growth.
- **Manifestation:** Focus on the egg as a symbol of nurturing new ideas or projects.

5. Coprolites (Fossilized Dinosaur Dung)

Description: Fossilized dinosaur dung, known as coprolites, provides insight into ancient diets and ecosystems.
Symbolism: Nourishment, transformation, and renewal.
Magickal Uses:

- **Grounding and Renewal:** Use coprolites in rituals to cleanse old energy and foster growth.
- **Earth Connection:** Incorporate into Earth-based spells for grounding and fertility.
- **Cleansing:** Representing the natural cycle of decay and renewal, coprolites can be used to banish negativity.

6. Fossilized Tracks (Trace Fossils)

Description: Fossilized footprints and trackways left by dinosaurs as they moved through their environment.
Symbolism: Movement, journey, and purpose.
Magickal Uses:

- **Guidance Spells:** Use track fossils to find clarity and direction in life.
- **Pathfinding:** Place on your altar when seeking guidance on a significant decision.
- **Life Transitions:** Incorporate into rituals to represent progress and forward motion.

7. Amber with Inclusions

Description: Fossilized tree resin often containing preserved prehistoric insects, plants, or other organic materials.

Symbolism: Preservation, memory, and spiritual connection.

Magickal Uses:

- **Memory and Ancestral Work:** Use amber to connect with the energies of the past or ancestral wisdom.
- **Protection:** Wear or carry amber to create a protective shield against harm.
- **Healing:** Incorporate into healing rituals for emotional balance and renewal.

8. Fossilized Plants

Description: Fossils of ancient plants, such as ferns or trees, symbolize life cycles and Earth's fertility.

Symbolism: Growth, nurturing, and Earth energy.

Magickal Uses:

- **Growth Rituals:** Use plant fossils in spells to encourage personal or professional development.
- **Connection to Nature:** Meditate with plant fossils to deepen your bond with the Earth.
- **Healing Spells:** Incorporate into rituals for physical and emotional healing.

Using Fossils in Spellcraft

Fossils can be used in a variety of ways to enhance your magickal practice:

1. Altar Enhancements

- Place fossils on your altar to invoke their energy and symbolism during rituals.
- Create thematic altars with fossils that align with specific intentions (e.g., eggs for new beginnings, teeth for protection).

2. Talismans and Amulets

- Carry small fossils as personal talismans for protection, grounding, or empowerment.
- Wear fossilized amber or bone jewelry to keep the energy of prehistoric Earth close to you.

3. Ritual Tools

- Use fossils as focal points in meditation or spellwork.
- Incorporate fossilized claws or teeth into wands or staffs for added potency.

4. Elemental Magick

- Represent the element of Earth in your rituals with fossils.
- Use fossilized amber to connect with the element of fire through its resinous origins.

5. Meditation and Visualization

- Hold a fossil during meditation to connect with its energy and symbolism.
- Visualize the fossil's journey through time, drawing strength and wisdom from its endurance.

Cleansing and Charging Fossils

Before using fossils in your magickal practice, cleanse and charge them to remove residual energy and align them with your intentions:

Cleansing Methods:

- **Smoke Cleansing:** Pass the fossil through the smoke of sage, cedar, or palo santo.
- **Moonlight:** Place the fossil under the light of the Full Moon to cleanse and recharge.
- **Earth Burial:** Bury the fossil in soil for 24 hours to reconnect it with Earth's energy.

Charging Methods:

- **Visualization:** Hold the fossil and visualize it glowing with vibrant energy.
- **Intentional Placement:** Place the fossil on your altar with a candle or crystal aligned with your intention.

Choosing the Right Fossil for Your Practice

Consider the following when selecting fossils for spellcraft:

1. **Purpose:** Match the fossil type with your specific intention or need.
2. **Connection:** Choose fossils that resonate with you personally, whether through their appearance, energy, or history.
3. **Availability:** While genuine fossils are ideal, replicas or symbolic representations can also be effective if charged with intention.

Closing Thoughts on Fossil Magick

Fossils are powerful magickal tools that connect us to Earth's ancient past while guiding us in the present. By understanding their meanings and applications, you can incorporate their energy into your practice to enhance your connection to the prehistoric world, foster transformation, and tap into timeless wisdom.

As you continue exploring **The Dino Grimoire**, let these fossils be your companions on the journey, grounding you in the enduring power of the prehistoric Earth.

Appendix C: Prehistoric Magick Resources

Prehistoric magick draws from the vast mysteries of Earth's ancient past, merging history, spirituality, and creativity. Expanding your understanding of this unique field requires access to specialized resources, including books, tools, and references that connect you to the energies of the prehistoric world. This appendix provides a curated list of recommended resources to deepen your practice and enhance your knowledge.

Recommended Books

These books provide valuable insights into prehistoric life, fossil studies, and the symbolic use of ancient energies in magickal practices:

1. Fossil and Prehistory Reference

- **"The Dinosaur Heresies" by Robert T. Bakker**
  Description: A groundbreaking exploration of dinosaur behavior, biology, and evolution.
  Use in Magick: Offers a deeper understanding of dinosaurs' lives, enhancing their symbolic resonance in rituals.
- **"Prehistoric Life: The Definitive Visual History of Life on Earth" by DK Publishing**
  Description: A richly illustrated guide to the history of life on Earth, from the earliest microorganisms to the age of mammals.
  Use in Magick: Use this as a reference to align your practice with specific prehistoric eras or creatures.
- **"Dinosaurs: A Visual Encyclopedia" by DK Publishing**
  Description: An accessible guide to different species of dinosaurs and their characteristics.
  Use in Magick: A quick reference for choosing dinosaurs to represent specific magickal intentions.

2. Magickal and Spiritual Resources

- **"Earth Power: Techniques of Natural Magick" by Scott Cunningham**
  Description: A classic text on working with natural elements in magickal practices.
  Use in Magick: Adapt its techniques to incorporate fossils, stones, and prehistoric symbols into Earth-based rituals.
- **"The Book of Stones: Who They Are and What They Teach" by Robert Simmons and Naisha Ahsian**
  Description: A comprehensive guide to crystals and stones, including their energetic proper-

ties.

Use in Magick: Use this to understand how fossils and stones like amber, petrified wood, and coprolites can be used in prehistoric magick.

- **"The Magick of Rocks and Stones" by Cassandra Eason**
  Description: A resource for integrating stones and fossils into spiritual practices.
  Use in Magick: Discover rituals and spells that amplify the power of fossilized materials.

3. Mythology and Symbolism

- **"The Power of Myth" by Joseph Campbell**
  Description: An exploration of mythological archetypes and their role in human spirituality.
  Use in Magick: Apply Campbell's ideas to understand the archetypal power of dinosaurs and their place in prehistoric lore.
- **"The Golden Bough" by Sir James George Frazer**
  Description: A classic study of myth, ritual, and the cycles of life and death.
  Use in Magick: Incorporate its insights into rituals focused on transformation and rebirth.

Magickal Tools

1. Fossils

- **Amber with Inclusions:** Preserved prehistoric energy, ideal for protection and connection to ancient wisdom.
- **Petrified Wood:** A grounding and stabilizing tool for Earth-based magick.
- **Dinosaur Teeth or Bones:** Authentic fossils or replicas for strength, protection, and ancestral connection.

2. Crystals

- **Smoky Quartz:** Enhances grounding and protection during prehistoric magick rituals.
- **Labradorite:** A stone of transformation, ideal for working with extinction and renewal energies.
- **Malachite:** Supports growth and adaptability, mirroring the resilience of prehistoric life.

3. Ritual Supplies

- **Drums and Rattles:** Use for recreating the primal sounds of prehistoric Earth, enhancing ritual vibrations.
- **Animal Totem Cards or Dinosaur-Themed Oracle Decks:** Tools for connecting with the symbolic energy of specific dinosaurs.
- **Candles:** Color-coded candles (e.g., green for growth, black for transformation) to align with your magickal intentions.

Digital Resources

1. Websites

- **FossilEra (https://www.fossilera.com/)**
  Description: An online store for fossils, minerals, and crystals.
  Use in Magick: Source authentic fossils for use in your prehistoric magick practice.
- **The Dinosaur Database (https://www.dinodatabase.com/)**
  Description: A comprehensive resource for researching dinosaur species.
  Use in Magick: Gain detailed information about specific dinosaurs to align their traits with your rituals.
- **Mindat.org (https://www.mindat.org/)**
  Description: A database of minerals and geological formations.
  Use in Magick: Learn about fossilized stones and their properties for magickal applications.

2. Online Communities

- **Reddit Communities:**
  - *r/Magick:* Share prehistoric magick ideas and seek advice from experienced practitioners.
  - *r/Dinosaurs:* Engage with enthusiasts to deepen your knowledge of prehistoric life.
- **Facebook Groups:**
  - *Fossil Enthusiasts:* Connect with fossil collectors and acquire rare specimens.
  - *Magickal Practitioners:* Find communities focused on Earth-based and nature magick.

Workshops and Experiences
1. Fossil-Hunting Tours
Participate in guided fossil-hunting experiences to connect directly with prehistoric Earth's energy. Popular locations include:

- **Badlands National Park (South Dakota, USA):** Known for dinosaur fossils.
- **Isle of Wight (England):** A famous location for finding fossils from the Cretaceous period.
- **Dinosaur Provincial Park (Alberta, Canada):** A UNESCO World Heritage Site rich in prehistoric remains.

2. Museum Visits
Explore natural history museums to study fossils and gain inspiration for your magickal practices:

- **The American Museum of Natural History (New York, USA)**
- **The Natural History Museum (London, England)**
- **Royal Tyrrell Museum of Palaeontology (Alberta, Canada)**

3. Online Courses

- **Introduction to Paleontology (Coursera):** Learn about prehistoric life and fossils through accessible online classes.
- **Crystal and Stone Magick Workshops (Udemy):** Discover techniques for integrating fossilized stones into your spiritual practice.

Magickal Journals and Logs
Keep track of your experiences and findings with tools designed for magickal practitioners:

- **The Dino Grimoire Journal:** A customizable journal to document your prehistoric magick rituals, spells, and insights.
- **Spell Logs:** Create a dedicated space for recording fossil-based rituals and their outcomes.

Multimedia Resources
Documentaries

- **"Walking with Dinosaurs" (BBC Series)**
  Description: A visually stunning exploration of the lives of dinosaurs.
  Use in Magick: Visualize the energy and traits of specific dinosaurs during meditation or rituals.
- **"Prehistoric Planet" (Apple TV+)**
  Description: A modern take on prehistoric ecosystems and dinosaur behavior.
  Use in Magick: Gain inspiration for creating prehistoric-themed sacred spaces.

Podcasts

- **"I Know Dino"**
  Description: A podcast for dinosaur enthusiasts.
  Use in Magick: Discover in-depth information about dinosaur species to incorporate into your practice.
- **"The Dirt Podcast"**
  Description: Focused on archaeology and paleontology.
  Use in Magick: Gain insight into how ancient cultures viewed fossils and prehistoric life.

Final Thoughts on Prehistoric Magick Resources
The world of prehistoric magick is vast, offering endless opportunities for exploration and connection. By utilizing the resources in this guide, you can deepen your understanding of the ancient Earth, refine your magickal practice, and create meaningful rituals that honor the wisdom and power of prehistoric life.

Let these tools and references empower your journey through **The Dino Grimoire**, ensuring that the spirit of the prehistoric world remains alive in your magickal path.

<u>Message from the Author:</u>

I hope you enjoyed this book, I love astrology and knew there was not a book such as this out on the shelf. I love metaphysical items as well. Please check out my other books:

-Life of Government Benefits

-My life of Hell

-My life with Hydrocephalus

-Red Sky

-World Domination:Woman's rule

-World Domination:Woman's Rule 2: The War

-Life and Banishment of Apophis: book 1

-The Kidney Friendly Diet

-The Ultimate Hemp Cookbook

-Creating a Dispensary(legally)

-Cleanliness throughout life: the importance of showering from childhood to adulthood.

-Strong Roots: The Risks of Overcoddling children

-Hemp Horoscopes: Cosmic Insights and Earthly Healing

- Celestial Hemp Navigating the Zodiac: Through the Green Cosmos

-Astrological Hemp: Aligning The Stars with Earth's Ancient Herb

-The Astrological Guide to Hemp: Stars, Signs, and Sacred Leaves

-Green Growth: Innovative Marketing Strategies for your Hemp Products and Dispensary

-Cosmic Cannabis

-Astrological Munchies

-Henry The Hemp

-Zodiacal Roots: The Astrological Soul Of Hemp

- **Green Constellations: Intersection of Hemp and Zodiac**

-Hemp in The Houses: An astrological Adventure Through The Cannabis Galaxy

-Galactic Ganja Guide

Heavenly Hemp

Zodiac Leaves

Doctor Who Astrology

Cannastrology

Stellar Satvias and Cosmic Indicas

<u>Celestial Cannabis: A Zodiac Journey</u>

AstroHerbology: The Sky and The Soil: Volume 1

AstroHerbology:Celestial Cannabis:Volume 2

Cosmic Cannabis Cultivation

The Starry Guide to Herbal Harmony: Volume 1

The Starry Guide to Herbal Harmony: Cannabis Universe: Volume 2

Yugioh Astrology: Astrological Guide to Deck, Duels and more

Nightmare Mansion: Echoes of The Abyss

Nightmare Mansion 2: Legacy of Shadows

Nightmare Mansion 3: Shadows of the Forgotten

Nightmare Mansion 4: Echoes of the Damned

The Life and Banishment of Apophis: Book 2

Nightmare Mansion: Halls of Despair

Healing with Herb: Cannabis and Hydrocephalus

Planetary Pot: Aligning with Astrological Herbs: Volume 1

Fast Track to Freedom: 30 Days to Financial Independence Using AI, Assets, and Agile Hustles

Cosmic Hemp Pathways

How to Become Financially Free in 30 Days: 10,000 Paths to Prosperity

Zodiacal Herbage: Astrological Insights: Volume 1

Nightmare Mansion: Whispers in the Walls

The Daleks Invade Atlantis

Henry the hemp and Hydrocephalus

10X The Kidney Friendly Diet

Cannabis Universe: Adult coloring book

Hemp Astrology: The Healing Power of the Stars

Zodiacal Herbage: Astrological Insights: Cannabis Universe: Volume 2

Planetary Pot: Aligning with Astrological Herbs: Cannabis Universes: Volume 2

Doctor Who Meets the Replicators and SG-1: The Ultimate Battle for Survival

Nightmare Mansion: Curse of the Blood Moon

The Celestial Stoner: A Guide to the Zodiac

Cosmic Pleasures: Sex Toy Astrology for Every Sign

Hydrocephalus Astrology: Navigating the Stars and Healing Waters

Lapis and the Mischievous Chocolate Bar

Celestial Positions: Sexual Astrology for Every Sign

Apophis's Shadow Work Journal: : A Journey of Self-Discovery and Healing

Kinky Cosmos: Sexual Kink Astrology for Every Sign

Digital Cosmos: The Astrological Digimon Compendium

Stellar Seeds: The Cosmic Guide to Growing with Astrology

Apophis's Daily Gratitude Journal

Cat Astrology: Feline Mysteries of the Cosmos

The Cosmic Kama Sutra: An Astrological Guide to Sexual Positions

Unleash Your Potential: A Guided Journal Powered by AI Insights
Whispers of the Enchanted Grove

Cosmic Pleasures: An Astrological Guide to Sexual Kinks
369, 12 Manifestation Journal
Whisper of the nocturne journal(blank journal for writing or drawing)
The Boogey Book
Locked In Reflection: A Chastity Journey Through Locktober
Generating Wealth Quickly:
How to Generate $100,000 in 24 Hours
Star Magic: Harness the Power of the Universe
The Flatulence Chronicles: A Fart Journal for Self-Discovery
The Doctor and The Death Moth
Seize the Day: A Personal Seizure Tracking Journal
The Ultimate Boogeyman Safari: A Journey into the Boogie World and Beyond
Whispers of Samhain: 1,000 Spells of Love, Luck, and Lunar Magic: Samhain Spell Book
Apophis's guides:
Witch's Spellbook Crafting Guide for Halloween
<u>Frost & Flame: The Enchanted Yule Grimoire of 1000 Winter Spells</u>
<u>The Ultimate Boogey Goo Guide & Spooky Activities for Halloween Fun</u>
Harmony of the Scales: A Libra's Spellcraft for Balance and Beauty
The Enchanted Advent: 36 Days of Christmas Wonders

Nightmare Mansion: The Labyrinth of Screams
Harvest of Enchantment: 1,000 Spells of Gratitude, Love, and Fortune for Thanksgiving
The Boogey Chronicles: A Journal of Nightly Encounters and Shadowy Secrets
The 12 Days of Financial Freedom: A Step-by-Step Christmas Countdown to Transform Your Finances
Sigil of the Eternal Spiral Blank Journal
A Christmas Feast: Timeless Recipes for Every Meal
Holiday Stress-Free Solutions: A Survival Guide to Thriving During the Festive Season
Yu-Gi-Oh! Holiday Gifting Mastery: The Ultimate Guide for Fans and Newcomers Alike
Holiday Harmony: A Hydrocephalus Survival Guide for the Festive Season
Celestial Craft: The Witch's Almanac for 2025 – A Cosmic Guide to Manifestations, Moons, and Mystical Events
Doctor Who: The Toymaker's Winter Wonderland
Tulsa King Unveiled: A Thrilling Guide to Stallone's Mafia Masterpiece
Pendulum Craft: A Complete Guide to Crafting and Using Personalized Divination Tools
Nightmare Mansion: Santa's Eternal Eve
Starlight Noel: A Cosmic Journey through Christmas Mysteries
The Dark Architect: Unlocking the Blueprint of Existence

If you want solar for your home go here: https://www.harborsolar.live/apophisenterprises/

Get Some Tarot cards: https://www.makeplayingcards.com/sell/apophis-occult-shop

Get some shirts: https://www.bonfire.com/store/apophis-shirt-emporium/

<u>**Instagrams:**</u>
@apophis_enterprises,
@apophisbookemporium,
@apophisscardshop
Twitter: @apophisenterpr1
Tiktok:@apophisenterprise
Youtube: @sg1fan23477, @FiresideRetreatKingdom
Hive: @sg1fan23477
CheeLee: @SG1fan23477

Podcast: **Apophis** **Chat** **Zone:** https://open.spotify.com/show/5zXbr-CLEV2xzCp8ybrfHsk?si=fb4d4fdbdce44dec

Newsletter: https://apophiss-newsletter-27c897.beehiiv.com/